Colonial America: A Very Short Introduction

VERY SHORT INTRODUCTIONS are for anyone wanting a stimulating and accessible way in to a new subject. They are written by experts and have been published in more than 25 languages worldwide.

The series began in 1995 and now represents a wide variety of topics in history, philosophy, religion, science, and the humanities. The VSI library now contains more than 300 volumes—a Very Short Introduction to everything from ancient Egypt and Indian philosophy to conceptual art and cosmology—and will continue to grow in a variety of disciplines.

Very Short Introductions available now:

Available soon:

For more information visit our web site

www.oup.co.uk/general/vsi/

Alan Taylor

COLONIAL AMERICA

A Very Short Introduction

OXFORD
UNIVERSITY PRESS

OXFORD
UNIVERSITY PRESS

Oxford University Press is a department of the University of Oxford.
It furthers the University's objective of excellence in
research, scholarship, and education by publishing worldwide.

Oxford   New York

Auckland   Cape Town   Dar es Salaam   Hong Kong   Karachi
Kuala Lumpur   Madrid   Melbourne   Mexico City   Nairobi
New Delhi   Shanghai   Taipei   Toronto

With offices in

Argentina   Austria   Brazil   Chile   Czech Republic   France   Greece
Guatemala   Hungary   Italy   Japan   Poland   Portugal   Singapore
South Korea   Switzerland   Thailand   Turkey   Ukraine   Vietnam

Published in the United States of America by
Oxford University Press
198 Madison Avenue, New York, NY 10016

Library of Congress Cataloging-in-Publication Data
Taylor, Alan, 1955–
Colonial America : a very short introduction / Alan Taylor.
p.   cm. — (Very short introductions)
Includes bibliographical references and index.
ISBN 978-0-19-976623-9 (pbk. : acid-free paper)
1. North America—History. 2. Europe—Colonies—America—History.
3. Indians of North America—History. 4. North America—History—
Colonial period, ca. 1600–1775. 5. Indians of North America—History—
Colonial period, ca. 1600–1775. I. Title.
E45.T39   2012   973.2—dc23   2012029104

1 3 5 7 9 8 6 4 2

Printed in Great Britain
by Ashford Colour Press Ltd., Gosport, Hants.
on acid-free paper

For John Demos

Contents

List of illustrations

Acknowledgments

At Oxford University Press, I am grateful to Nancy Toff for expert editing and savvy guidance; and to Emily Sacharin and Sonia Tycko for patient and deft assistance. I am also indebted to Jane Kamensky and Peter Wood, and two anonymous reviewers who so generously and insightfully commented on the manuscript, which is much improved from their efforts. I have dedicated the book to John Demos, who many years ago, when at Brandeis University, introduced me to the study of the colonial era and its diverse peoples. I have greatly benefitted from his example, scholarship, and keen insights—on the Red Sox of today as well as the human dramas of the past.

Introduction: Maps

In 1721 at Charles Town (now Charleston) in South Carolina, the colonial governor, Sir Francis Nicholson, met a visiting delegation of Indian chiefs from villages in the Piedmont. Later known as "Catawbas," they thought of themselves as belonging to a loose confederation of eleven villages. The chiefs gave the governor a deerskin decorated with a map that represented their villages as a network of linked circles. We now know the map from two paper copies made by Nicholson's secretary and sent to England. The copyist added the English language labels: translations and representations of the explanations orally conveyed by the chiefs when they delivered their gift.

Rather than represent natives as one common mass of Indians, the map introduced the governor to a complex network of diverse peoples. At the privileged center of the map, the maker represented the eleven Catawba villages as named circles: Casuie, Charra, Nasaw, Nustie, Saxippaha, Succa, Suttirie, Wasmisa, Waterie, Wiapie, and Youchine. The map also names two more-familiar native peoples—the Cherokee and Chickasaw—but sets them on the fringe. The map warns us to beware of how much nuance we lose when lumping the many native peoples together as Indians.

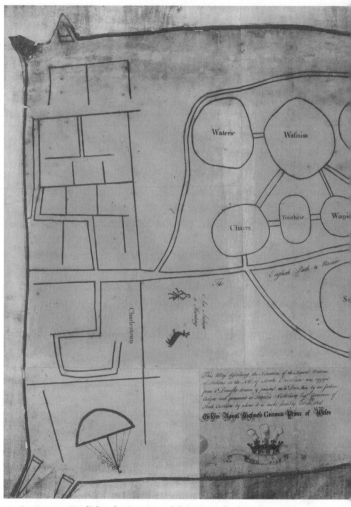

Within the map, the following labels appear:

Waterie

Wasmisa

Youchine

Wiapie

Chuwn

English Path to Nasaw

Charlestown

This Map describing the Scituation of the several Nations of Indians to the NW of South Carolina was copyed from a Draught drawn & painted on a Deer Skin by an Indian Cacique and presented to Francis Nicholson Esqr Governour of South Carolina by whom it is most humbly Dedicated

To His Royal Highness GEORGE Prince of Wales

1. In 1721, an English colonist created this copy of a deerskin map of South Carolina's Piedmont region, originally drawn by a group of Catawba chiefs. The map places eleven Catawba villages in the center of a complex network of native people.

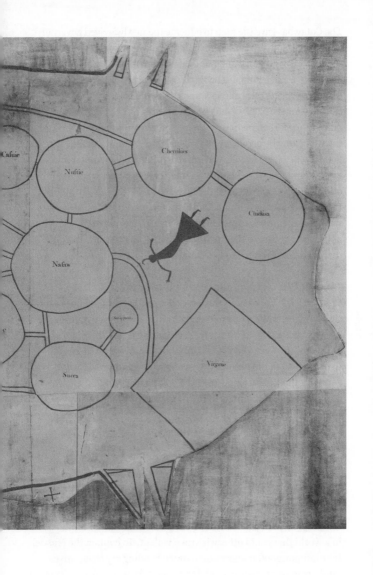

Cafuie

Nuftie

Cherrikes

Chickisa

Nafaw

Weroaqueoc

Virginie

Sucra

The Catawbas gave the map to educate the newly arrived governor to native diplomacy. Rather than depict geographical proportions, the map conveys social and political relationships between peoples, both native and colonial. The thirteen native peoples appear as circles of varying sizes and locations, with the largest and the most central—for the Nasaw—enjoying a pride of place. By omitting many other Indian peoples in the region, the map assured Nicholson that the Catawba peoples, and especially the Nasaw, were his special and indispensable friends who served as his proper conduit into the wider native world of the vast interior. Of course, maps made by other native peoples altered the hierarchy and centrality of villages. In 1723 Nicholson collected a similar map made by the Chickasaws, who gave themselves centrality with strong links to the Choctaw and Cherokee and to the English at Charles Town, but with only a marginal place allotted to the Catawba.

The 1721 Catawba map also represents only two colonial polities: Charles Town appears on the left as a cross-hatching of lines at right-angles, while a box named "Virginia" occupies the lower right corner. Living in oval wigwams in circular villages surrounded by palisades, the Catawba felt spiritually safest in rounded forms, which reflected the natural cycles of seasons and lives. In stark contrast, the Indians identified the colonists with their square and rectangular buildings in towns platted as grids: alien and unnatural forms that seemed odd. The well-rounded natives thought of the newcomers as squares.

The map represents an Indian bid to incorporate the newcomers into a native nexus of diplomacy and trade in the hope that the colonists could learn how to coexist in a shared land. Parallel lines connect both Charles Town and Virginia to the native circles. The lines represented paths of safe conduct for traders and diplomats in a world that could otherwise turn violent. To contact the Nustie, for example, good manners demanded sending representatives (and presents of trade goods) first to the Nasaw. Far from accepting subordination to the Virginians or the Carolinians, the Nasaw cast themselves as the brokers of commerce and power in a world dominated by native peoples and conducted in native ways. In this map, Indians hold the center, while the colonists remain marginal.

The self-assurance of the map jars our conventional assumptions about colonial history, which casts Indians as primitive, marginal, and doomed. We do not expect to find natives acting as the self-confident teachers of colonists cast as rather obtuse, but redeemable, students. Indeed, the map offers an alternative vision of coexistence on native terms.

In the lower left-hand corner, near Charles Town, the map seems to depict a deployed parachute. But modern eyes trick us into assuming that the subsequent English labels define a consistent up and down (or north and south). In fact, the Nasaw intended viewers to circle around the map to view it from every angle without privileging any one side. The apparent parachute is, instead, a ship with a central mast mounted by a pennant and linked by ropes to the deck. In addition to a grid of streets, Charles Town impressed natives as a harbor filled with ships capable of crossing the Atlantic. Ultimately, the map represents the meeting of two different but increasingly interpenetrated networks: the native-made circles and paths of the interior, and the colonial entrepôts of transatlantic commerce.

Brought together in 1721, the Catawba map-givers and the English colonial governor jointly speak to the efforts by historians in recent years to grasp the interplay of the "Atlantic" and "Continental" dimensions of colonial history. "Atlantic historians" examine the interdependence of Europe, Africa, and the Americas through the transatlantic flows of goods, people, plants, animals, capital, and ideas. "Continental historians" seek to restore the importance of native peoples to the colonial story. Rather than treat Indians as unchanging and doomed primitives, the continental approach emphasizes the natives' ability to adapt to the newcomers and to compel concessions from them.

The new combination of Atlantic and continental history challenges the older history of colonial America that emphasized the English cultural "seeds," first planted at Jamestown in Virginia in 1607 and at Plymouth in New England in 1620. According to the older view, "American history" began in the east in the English colonies and spread westward into a vast continent without a prior history. In this old history, the continent's Indian peoples and Spanish and French colonies seemed relevant only as enemies, as challenges that brought out the best in the English as they remade themselves into Americans.

Known as "American exceptionalism," the old history offers a national origins myth, where common English colonists escaped from the rigid customs, social hierarchies, and constrained resources of Europe into an abundant land of both challenge and opportunity. Rising to the challenge, they prospered by working hard to turn the forest into farms. In the process, they became entrepreneurial and egalitarian individualists who could be ruled only by their own consent. Inevitably, they rebelled against British rule to form an independent and republican union of states destined to expand to the Pacific. American exceptionalism casts the colonial period simply as an Anglophone preparation for the United States, defined as a uniquely middle-class society and democracy.

There is some truth to the traditional picture, for many British colonists did find more land, greater prosperity, and higher status than they could have achieved by remaining in the mother country. And (save for in the West Indies) British America did lack the aristocrats of the mother country, creating a social vacuum that enabled successful lawyers, merchants, and planters to comprise a colonial elite that favored commercial values.

But American exceptionalism offers a selective story that obscures the heavy costs of colonization. Thousands of colonists found only intense labor and early graves owing to diseases and Indian hostility. And those who succeeded bought their good fortune by taking lands from Indians and by exploiting the labor of indentured servants and African slaves. Between 1492 and 1776, North America lost population, as diseases and wars killed Indians faster than colonists could replace them. During the eighteenth century, most colonial arrivals were African conscripts forcibly carried to a land of slavery, rather than European volunteers seeking a domain of freedom.

The traditional story also obscures the broad cultural and geographic range of colonial America, which extended far beyond the British colonies of the Atlantic seaboard. Many native peoples encountered colonizers not as westward-bound Englishmen but as Spanish heading north from Mexico, Russians coming eastward from Siberia, or as French probing the Great Lakes and the Mississippi River. Each of those colonial ventures interacted in distinctive ways with particular settings and diverse Indians to construct varied Americas—all of which contributed to the later United States. Colonial America was far more than a simple story of the English becoming Americans.

Colonial societies *did* diverge from their mother countries—but in a more complex and radical manner than imagined within the narrow vision of American uplift for English men. Colonial conditions produced an unprecedented mixing of African, European, and Indian cultures. The world had never known such a rapid and intense intermingling of peoples—and of microbes, plants, and animals from different continents. Everyone had to adapt to a new world wrought by those combinations.

The Indians also lived in a new world transformed by the intrusion of diverse newcomers bearing alien diseases, livestock, trade goods, weapons, and Christian beliefs. Resilient and resourceful, some natives seized opportunities to turn the new plants and animals to their own advantage. For example, on the Great Plains during the eighteenth century, the Indian peoples acquired horses that endowed them with a new mobility and prowess as buffalo hunters and mounted warriors. The mounted Indians defied colonial intrusions and even rolled back settlements along the southern Great Plains. Similarly, the Navajo people of the American Southwest became newly rich by appropriating European sheep and looms to their own ends, producing distinctive and beautiful wool cloth.

Because of their resilience, Indians became indispensable to the rival European empires in North America. On their contested frontiers, each empire needed Indians as trading partners, guides, religious converts, and military allies. By the late seventeenth century, the empires competed to construct networks of Indian allies—and tried to unravel those of the other powers.

We need to recall the very different cultural landscape of colonial America, where natives hoped to integrate the newcomers, who dwelt in a world of square buildings and properties, into a network of circles and paths. To understand the true sweep of colonial America and the pivotal importance of native peoples, multiply by a thousand the circles and the relational paths of the Nasaw map. Extend that array across the continent with links to British squares up and down the Atlantic seaboard; Spanish squares in Florida, Texas, New Mexico, and California; French squares in the Mississippi and St. Lawrence watersheds; and even Russian squares in the far northwest along the Aleutian islands and the Alaska coast. That dense and complex picture belies the imperial fantasies of textbook maps where the claims of vast European empires cover the continent, prematurely submerging the many native peoples. Indeed, it took four centuries of trial and error, struggle and setback for Euro-Americans to dominate the continent. During the long colonial era, the natives of the vast interior could oblige sojourning traders and soldiers to play by the rules of native diplomacy. Circles were not squares, but both had to share paths between them.

Chapter 1
Encounters

The settlement of North America began long before 1492 and came from Asia rather than Europe. About 15,000 to 12,000 years ago, the first Americans migrated from Siberia in northeast Asia. The migrants came in small groups that ranged far and wide in pursuit of the grazing herds of large, hairy, and meaty (but dangerous) mammals, including wooly mammoths. Armed with stone-tipped spears, the hunters either came in small, hide-covered boats working along the coast or walked into North America during an Ice Age that locked up more of the world's water in polar ice caps, lowering the ocean levels by about 360 feet and connecting Siberia to Alaska. Little did they realize that the bridge would vanish beneath the rising Pacific Ocean when the global climate warmed about 10,000 years ago. A second wave of migrants, Athapaskan speakers, followed about 9,000 years ago and eventually migrated to the American Southwest, where they became known as Apache and Navajo. A third wave arrived about 5,000 years ago, when the ancestors of the Inuit settled the Arctic coast of North America while their Aleut cousins occupied the islands south and west of Alaska.

Meanwhile, the descendants of the first pulse had spread southward and eastward across North America and beyond into South America. Known to scholars as "Paleo-Indians," they initially lived by hunting and gathering in small bands of about fifteen to fifty people. Thanks to an abundant diet of big game, the Paleo-Indian population grew rapidly. As bands became too large for a locale to sustain, they subdivided and most moved on. By about 9,000 years ago (perhaps earlier), natives had reached the southernmost tip of South America, about 8,000 miles from the Bering Strait.

Meanwhile, the global warming gradually shrank the arctic grasslands and expanded the temperate forests in North America. Climate change and the spread of highly skilled hunters combined to exterminate most of the largest mammals including the mammoths. Obliged to adapt, the nomadic bands adopted new and more diversified strategies to tap a broader range of food sources. Learning their local environments more intimately, they harvested a broader range of foods, including shellfish, fish, birds, nuts, seeds, berries, and tubers. Their hunting evolved into the patient and prolonged tracking of smaller, more mobile mammals: especially deer, antelope, moose, elk, and caribou. Gender structured roles as men fished and hunted while women harvested and prepared wild plants.

Marking the shift to a new way of life, archaeologists refer to the natives after 9,000 years ago as "Archaic" to distinguish them from their "Paleo-Indian" ancestors. By learning how to exploit a broader array of food sources, the Archaic Indians more than compensated for the loss of the great mammals. Obtaining more to eat and more reliably, those in North America multiplied from about 100,000 people to 1,000,000 between 9,000 and 3,000 years ago.

Compared to their Paleo-Indian ancestors, the Archaic Indians dwelled in larger groups within smaller territories. They developed more enduring villages located beside rivers and lakes or along seacoasts, places where fish and birds, shellfish, and wild food plants were most abundant. Each band developed a seasonal round of activity and movement within a more defined territory, harvesting those plants and animals as they became abundant at different seasons. For example, in the Southwest during the summer and fall the people dispersed to hunt rabbits, deer, elk, bighorn sheep, and antelope. The onset of the rainy winter led them to gather in the canyons, where they harvested prickly pear and piñon nuts. In the spring, they scattered again in pursuit of roots and berries and game.

As the Archaic Indian bands multiplied and spread into many distinct environmental niches, their cultures became more diverse with differing languages, rituals, mythic stories, and kinship systems. By 1492, the native peoples of North America spoke at least 375 distinct languages. But these peoples did not live in isolation from one another, for trade connected them over long distances. At sites in the Midwest or Great Basin, archaeologists find marine shells from the Atlantic and Pacific coasts; on the coasts they uncover copper from the Great Lakes and obsidian from the Rocky Mountains. Ideas and innovations passed along with the exchange of these objects so that the trading peoples influenced one another over long distances.

The leading innovation derived from Mesoamerica: south-central Mexico and central America. In Mesoamerica the natives pioneered the three great crops of North American horticulture—maize, squashes, and beans—about 3,000 years ago. Through trial and error over many generations, horticulture evolved as some Indian bands protected, watered, and harvested productive patches of wild plants with edible seeds. They also gradually developed hybrids of growing reliability and productivity. By expanding the food supply, horticulture permitted the native population to surge and to develop larger villages with a more complex and hierarchical society, for the food surplus enabled some people to specialize as craftsmen, merchants, priests, and rulers.

From Mesoamerica the new horticulture slowly spread northward, reaching the American Southwest by about 2,500 years ago, the

Southeast and Midwest about 2,000 years ago, and the Northeast by about 1,000 years ago. But horticulture never became universal in native North America, for many peoples stuck to the Archaic combination of hunting, gathering, and fishing. Some lived where the growing season was too short: in the vast arctic and subarctic regions of Alaska and Canada or in the high elevations of the Rockies and Sierra Nevada. Others dwelled where there was too little water: in the western Great Plains and in most of the Great Basin. For the hunting bands of the mountains, deserts, and subarctic, the great innovation of about 1,500 years ago was their adoption of the bow and arrow. Natives also did not adopt horticulture in the coastal zone of California and the Pacific Northwest—despite the long growing seasons and abundant water. Endowed by an especially abundant natural environment rich in fish, sea-mammals, and acorns, the native peoples of the Pacific coast could develop elaborate rituals, art, and status hierarchies without cultivating crops.

In the American Southwest, horticulture spawned the cultures known to scholars as the Hohokam and Anasazi. The Hohokam lived in the Gila and Salt River valleys of southern Arizona, while the Anasazi occupied upland canyons in the "Four Corners Region" (the intersection of Arizona, New Mexico, Utah, and Colorado). To compensate for the arid climate, the Hohokam built more than 500 miles of canals to irrigate thousands of acres devoted to their crops, while the Anasazi system caught and retained winter's rain on the mesa tops for spring and summer release to their low-lying fields beside the intermittent stream beds. Despite lacking beasts of burden, a system of writing, metal tools, or the wheel, the two cultures built substantial stone and adobe towns (later called *pueblos* by the Spanish) led by men who combined the roles of chief and priest.

During the twelfth century, the growing population strained the local resources in both the Hohokam and Anasazi countries. Many years of drought then set off a chain reaction of crop failure, malnutrition, and violent feuds over the dwindling resources. The hard work of supporting their chiefs and priests and maintaining the irrigation systems or the earthworks came to seem futile. During the thirteenth century, most of the Hohokam abandoned their towns to disperse into the hills, where they reverted to a mobile strategy of hunting and gathering, which shifted with the seasons. During the same century, most of the Anasazi fled south and east to found new pueblos, primarily beside the Rio Grande River, which offered enough year-round water to sustain irrigation even in drought years. Found there during the sixteenth century by the Spanish, they became known as the "Pueblo Indians."

In contrast to the Southwest, the vast Mississippi watershed enjoyed a humid and temperate climate. Consequently, the Mississippian peoples did not need irrigation systems to sustain their riverside fields of corn, maize, and squash. Drawing upon Mesoamerican models, some Mississippian peoples built large towns around central plazas, which featured earthen pyramids topped by wooden temples that doubled as the residences of chiefs, who claimed kinship to the sacred sun. The common people paid tribute in labor and crops to sustain their local chief who, in turn, often paid tribute to a paramount chief, who dwelled on top of the tallest pyramid in the region's largest town. Rivals for regional power, the chiefs waged wars that compelled the construction of immense wooden stockades around their towns.

The largest, wealthiest, and most complex town lay at Cahokia, on a fertile flood plain near the Mississippi River in Illinois just east of St. Louis. Developed between 900 and 1100, Cahokia and its suburbs covered about six square miles and had a population of at least 10,000 people. The central pyramid contained more than 800,000 cubic yards of earth, covered 16 acres, and rose 110 feet high. It was the third largest pyramid in North America, behind the two in central Mexico.

During the twelfth century, however, Cahokia lost population and power, and it was abandoned in the middle of the thirteenth

2. This aerial perspective shows Cahokia as it may have looked around 1150. The massive central pyramid ranked as the third largest pyramid in North America.

century—at the same time of crisis for the Anasazi and Hohokam. Here too the large population depleted local resources, particularly the game animals and the wood needed for fires, homes, and the defensive stockade. The deteriorating conditions discredited the paramount chief, which led to dissension within Cahokia and rebellions by the subordinated villages on the periphery. Most of the people dispersed to live in smaller villages without powerful chiefs.

Although the hierarchical Mississippian culture declined in its northern reaches around Cahokia, that culture remained vibrant to the south as far as the Gulf of Mexico, where, during the sixteenth century, Spanish explorers found crowded villages, tall pyramids, broad fields of maize, immense storehouses, dignified chiefs, and disciplined warriors. But those explorers introduced diseases that would, by the end of that century, deplete and disperse the Mississippian peoples.

During the late fifteenth and early sixteenth centuries, Europeans had developed the maritime technology and the imperial ambitions to explore and dominate the world's oceans. Long a barrier to Europeans, the Atlantic Ocean became their route to the immense lands and many peoples of the great beyond. Between 1450 and 1500 in dozens of voyages, European mariners found the Americas and rounded Africa to cross the Indian Ocean to India and the East Indies. In 1519–1522 Spanish sailors first circumnavigated the globe, confirming that the oceans formed an integrated system, which European ships could probe. On distant coasts, the mariners established fortified outposts to dominate local trade, as the Europeans created the first transoceanic, global empires. It was an extraordinary and unprecedented burst of geographic understanding, daring, and enterprise.

The new discoveries and their exploitation transformed Europe from a parochial backwater into the world's most dynamic and powerful continent. Previously the European Christians had felt hemmed in by their rivals and neighbors the Muslims, who subscribed to the world's other, great expansionist faith. During the fifteenth century, the Muslim world was larger, wealthier, more powerful, and more scientifically advanced than European Christendom. The Muslim realms extended across North Africa and around the southern and eastern Mediterranean Sea to embrace the Balkans, the Near East, Central Asia, and Southeast Asia. European Christians longed to break out and circumvent the Muslim world in search of the trade riches of sub-Saharan Africa (gold and ivory) and East Asia (silks, gems, and spices).

In the exception that proved the rule, on the Iberian Peninsula the kingdoms of Aragon, Castile, and Portugal gradually rolled back the Muslim Moors. In 1469 the marriage of Queen Isabella and Prince Ferdinand united Aragon and Castile to create "Spain." Especially zealous, able, and expansionist monarchs, Isabella and Ferdinand completed the *reconquista* (reconquest) of Iberia in

1492. That long and violent struggle had developed a crusading spirit led by a militant clergy and an ambitious warrior caste known as the *hidalgos*.

Close to Africa and facing the Atlantic, Spain and Portugal were well-situated to lead the maritime expansion of Europe. During the fifteenth century, the Spanish and Portuguese developed the larger ships and new navigation techniques needed to undertake longer voyages beyond the Mediterranean into the rougher waters of the Atlantic. Proceeding incrementally, mariners probed along the northwest coast of Africa, discovering along the way three sets of islands in the eastern Atlantic: the Canaries, Azores, and Madeiras. The Atlantic islands provided the safe harbors, valuable timber, and fertile soils that attracted Iberian colonists. Only the Canaries had natives. Known as the Guanches, the Canary Islanders were an olive-complexioned people related to the Berbers of nearby North Africa.

Conditioned by the *reconquista*, the Iberians insisted that the Guanches deserved to be conquered and enslaved because they were neither civilized nor Christian. After pushing aside the Portuguese competition, the Spanish completed their conquest of the Canaries during the 1490s. New diseases and Spanish victories destroyed the Guanches. The conquerors replaced the Guanches with free colonists and with slaves imported from Africa. In the fifteenth-century Canaries, we find the training grounds for the Spanish invasion of the Americas.

The Portuguese continued their probes south and east around Africa, into the Indian Ocean, and across to India, the gateway to the trade riches of the East. Excluded from that trade by Portuguese hostility, the Spanish looked westward across the Atlantic in search of a direct route to the coast of China. They followed the visionary theory of Christopher Columbus, an ambitious mariner from Genoa in Italy. In 1492, with three ships navigated by about ninety men, Columbus sailed southwest from

Spain to the Canaries and across the Atlantic to a landfall in the Bahama Islands, just east of Florida. Turning south, Columbus encountered the West Indies—the islands that framed the Caribbean Sea. Supposing that he had found the East Indies, near the coast of Asia, Columbus insisted that the native peoples were "Indians," a misnomer that has stuck.

Sailing home, Columbus dazzled the monarchs with his glowing reports of the Indians' gold jewelry and their supposed proximity to Asia. In September 1493 Columbus returned to Hispaniola, one of the West Indies, with seventeen ships, 1,200 men, sugarcane plants, and livestock. The Spanish were coming to stay, to dominate the land and its natives, and to weave the new lands into an empire based in Europe. Columbus also continued to explore around the Caribbean Sea, discovering more islands and the long coast of South America, but he died in 1506 stubbornly clinging to a conviction that his discoveries lay close to the coast of Asia. Consequently, "America" would be named for another Genoese mariner, Amerigo Vespucci, who recognized that the lands were a New World far from Asia.

Meanwhile, Spanish colonization destroyed the Taíno people of Hispaniola. From a population of at least 300,000 in 1492, the islanders declined to about 33,000 by 1510 and to a mere 500 by 1548. Like the Guanche, the Taíno died primarily from virulent new diseases unintentionally introduced by the Spanish, but the colonizers compounded the destructive impact of the diseases by callous exploitation, for the Spanish forced the Taíno to labor on colonial mines, ranches, and plantations where they suffered and died from a brutal work regimen. Natives who resisted reaped destructive and deadly raids on their villages. The refugees starved in the densely forested hills. Dislocated, traumatized, overworked, and underfed people proved especially vulnerable to disease. In sum, the natives suffered from a deadly combination of microparasitism by disease pathogens *and* macroparasitism by Spanish colonizers.

During the next two centuries, throughout the Americas, the explorers and colonists repeatedly reported horrifying and unprecedented epidemics among the native peoples. The waves of epidemics reduced the native population to about one-tenth of its precontact numbers by 1700. Recognizing this demographic catastrophe, recent scholars have dramatically revised upward their estimates of the Pre-Columbian population in the Americas: in 1492 the Americas held approximately 50 to 100 million people, of whom about 5 to 10 million lived north of Mexico. That revised understanding of a well-populated North America belies the former characterization of the continent as a "virgin land" virtually untouched by humans and longing for European settlement.

The exchange of infectious diseases between the invaders and the natives was remarkably one-sided. Apparently only one major disease—venereal syphilis—passed from the Americas into Europe with the returning explorers and sailors. Although painful and sometimes fatal, syphilis did not kill enough people to stem Europe's population growth during the sixteenth century.

Before 1492 the Native Americans had plenty of diseases, but they proved less virulent than those that had developed in the Old World of Europe, Asia, and Africa after the Paleo-Indians had emigrated to the Americas. The newer Eurasian diseases included smallpox, typhus, diphtheria, bubonic plague, malaria, yellow fever, cholera, and influenza. Their deadly evolution derived, in part, from the close proximity of Old World peoples to their domesticated mammals—particularly pigs—with which they shared microscopic parasites. New and especially powerful diseases developed as viruses shifted back and forth between the species. In contrast, North American natives domesticated only one mammal—the dog—which rarely shares pathogens with its best friends.

Beginning in 1492, Europeans suddenly carried their more virulent diseases to the American continents where the natives lacked the immunological resistance of past experience. During the sixteenth and seventeenth centuries, the colonizers did not intentionally disseminate disease. Indeed, they did not yet know how to do so, for they knew nothing of microbes or that some caused disease. Instead, they attributed epidemics to a divine judgment by an angry God. And the Spanish regretted the epidemics because they valued Indians as coerced labor to work on mines, plantations, ranches, and farms. Beginning on Hispaniola in 1518, the Spanish had to import thousands of slaves from West Africa to replace the dying Indians on the new plantations around the Caribbean.

The forced marriage of the two hemispheres meant a demographic boom for Europe but a demographic disaster for the Americas. The Native American proportion of the global population collapsed from about 7 percent in 1492 to less than 1 percent in 1800. At the same time, Europe's population more than doubled from 80 million in 1492 to 180 million by 1800. That growth increased Europe's share in the world's population from about 11 percent in 1492 to 20 percent in 1800.

The growth in Europe depended on an increased supply of food because better-fed people survive to reproduce in larger numbers. That improved diet derived primarily from the European adoption of highly productive new food crops first cultivated in the Americas. Superior in their horticulture, the natives had domesticated plants that had higher yields than their Old World counterparts. Measured as an average yield in calories per hectare (a hectare is 10,000 square meters, the equivalent of 2.5 acres), cassava (9.9 million), maize (7.3 million), and potatoes (7.5 million) trumped the traditional European grains: wheat (4.2), barley (5.1), and oats (5.5).

Planting New World seeds in the Old World soil dramatically expanded the food supply in Africa and Europe. The imported plants endowed farmers with larger yields on smaller plots. For example, it took at least five acres planted in grain to support a peasant family, but potatoes could subsist three families on the same amount of land. The new crops were also more flexible, enabling Old World farmers to cultivate soils hostile to their traditional grains. Unlike wheat, maize can grow in sandy soils and thrive in hot climes, while potatoes prosper in cold, thin, and damp soils unsuitable for any grain. In effect, maize and potatoes extended the amount of land that Old World farmers could cultivate. A tropical plant, cassava (also known as manioc), thrived in Africa after introduction during the sixteenth century. Maize spread eastward from Iberia around the Mediterranean to become fundamental to the peasant diet. Potato cultivation expanded in northern, central, and eastern Europe.

In effect, the post-Columbian exchanges reduced people on the American side of the Atlantic, while swelling those on the European and African shores. Eventually, the surplus population flowed westward to refill the demographic vacuum on the American half of the Atlantic world. That shift rendered the surviving natives a minority. By 1800 in present-day Canada and the United States, the 5 million Euro-Americans and 1 million African Americans already outnumbered the region's 600,000 natives.

The colonizers brought along plants and animals new to the Americas, some by design and others by accident. Determined to farm in a European manner, the colonists introduced their domesticated livestock—honeybees, pigs, horses, mules, sheep, and cattle—and their domesticated plants, including wheat, barley, rye, oats, grasses, and grapevines. But the colonists also inadvertently brought along weeds and rats. The imports spread rapidly and voraciously through the American landscape to the detriment of native plants, animals, and peoples. In sum, native peoples and their nature experienced an invasion, not just of foreign people but also of their associated livestock, vermin, and weeds. These worked in both synergy and competition to transform the environment, shaking the nature previously known and made by the natives.

Allowed to range widely, the cattle and pigs consumed wild plants and animals that the natives relied on for subsistence. The livestock also invaded the cultivated fields of the natives to consume the precious maize, beans, and squash. When Indians killed and ate trespassing animals, the colonists howled in protest and demanded compensation. If denied, angry colonists took revenge by raiding and burning Indian villages.

Despite the demographic disaster and the ecological changes, the Indians survived in sufficient numbers to hinder and slow the colonial conquest. Nowhere did the colonizers find a truly empty land. And nowhere was their ultimate triumph certain, for native peoples deftly adapted to their changing circumstances to defend their homes.

Chapter 2
New Spain

At the start of the sixteenth century, as the natives of Cuba and Hispaniola dwindled from disease and exploitation, the Spanish raided the mainland for new slaves to work their gold mines, cattle ranches, and sugar plantations. Because the new slaves proved just as short-lived as the Taíno, the demand for slave raiding widened, ravaging the native villages around the Caribbean and Gulf of Mexico from Venezuela to Florida.

From their captives, the Spanish learned of the rich and populous Aztec empire in central Mexico, featuring cities with stone temples and palaces, and a large population sustained by vast fields of maize, squashes, and beans. A rare empire among the natives, the Aztecs exacted tribute and forced labor from subject peoples over several hundred square miles. The tribute included victims for bloody sacrifice to the gods, for the Aztecs believed that only regular, ritual effusions of blood could sustain their rule and ensure the life-nourishing crops.

Allured by the reports of Aztec wealth, in 1519 the brilliant, ruthless, and charismatic Hernán Cortés led 600 armed volunteers, known as *conquistadores*, from Cuba to the coast of Mexico and into the interior, pushing through the hills to the great central valley. Alternating brutal displays of force with shrewd diplomacy, Cortés won support from the natives who had been subordinated by the Aztecs. The tributary Indians did not anticipate that the newcomers would eventually prove even more demanding masters than the hated Aztecs.

Hoping to tame Cortés and his men, the Aztec ruler Moctezuma invited the Spanish into his capital of Tenochtitlán as honored guests. The largest city in the Americas, Tenochtitlán had 200,000 inhabitants, nearly three times the number in Seville, Spain's premier city. The Spanish marveled at the immense palace of Moctezuma, the intricate system of canals, and the city's central plaza of tall, stone pyramid-temples. That wealth inflamed the Spanish desire to conquer, plunder, and enslave—which they justified in their hatred for the religious idols and human sacrifices of the Aztecs. The Spanish quickly turned Moctezuma into a shackled hostage and ultimately a corpse, as they provoked brutal street-fighting that eventually reduced Tenochtitlán to a bloody rubble. On the ruins, Cortés had enslaved Aztecs build a Spanish capital, Mexico City, which featured a great cathedral built from the reworked stones of the pyramids.

Other *conquistadores* extended the massive new empire through central America and deep into South America. During the 1530s, Francisco Pizarro with a mere 180 men conquered the Inca empire of Peru, practicing a ruthless brutality that might have shamed even Cortés.

How could a few hundred *conquistadores* so quickly and thoroughly overwhelm such formidable Indian empires? Although their guns were primitive, clumsy, and few, the *conquistadores* employed a steel technology of swords and pikes and crossbows superior to the stone-edged weapons of the natives. And the *conquistadores* with horses proved especially dreadful to the natives, who had never experienced the shocking power, speed, and height of mounted men wielding steel swords and lances. The Spanish also practiced a strategy of divide and conquer, finding local allies among subordinated Indian peoples who helped topple the dominant native power in each region. And the invaders benefited from the new diseases, which depleted and demoralized the resisting natives, who felt deserted by their gods and let down by their shamans.

The *conquistador* expeditions were private enterprises led by independent military contractors in pursuit of profit. The commander held a license from the Crown, which reserved one-fifth of the plunder and asserted sovereign jurisdiction over any conquered lands. Known as an *adelantado*, the commander recruited and financed his own expedition, with the help of investors who expected shares in the plunder. The commanders came from the Spanish gentry (*hidalgos*), while the rank-and-file soldiers were restless, young, single men from the middle ranks of Spanish society. Receiving no wages, they fought on speculation, gambling for a big score in plunder and slaves. The victorious commanders also obtained tribute annually paid by conquered Indian villages. Known as *encomienda*, this tribute came in the form of forced labor and annual produce paid to the *encomendero*.

The *conquistadores* insisted that their greed served other, more noble motives: to extend the realm of their monarch and to expand the church of their Christian God. They reasoned that riches were wasted on pagans and more properly bestowed upon Christian subjects of the Spanish rulers. By 1540, however, the Spanish Crown concluded that the *conquistadores* killed and enslaved too many Indians, wreaking a havoc that defied the imperial priority: to stabilize the natives as tax-paying Christian converts. During the 1540s, the Crown replaced the rule of the *conquistadores* with a bureaucracy comprised of lawyers and clerics.

At mid-century, the Crown divided the American empire into two immense administrative regions, known as viceroyalties, each led by a viceroy appointed by the king. The viceroyalty of New Spain consisted of Mexico, Central America, and the Caribbean Islands, while the viceroyalty of Peru included all of South America except Brazil, which the Portuguese had colonized. To watch and check

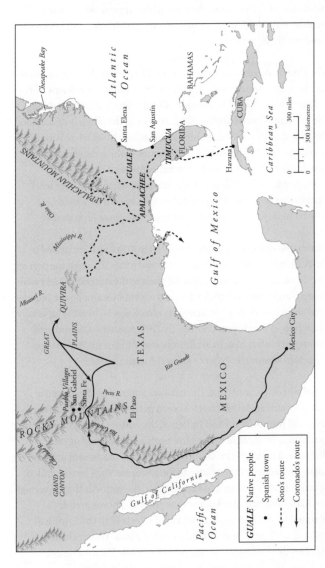

3. Northern New Spain, ca. 1580.

the power of the viceroys, the Crown also appointed a council of wealthy notables known as an *audiencia*, which drafted laws and conducted major trials.

The Crown also enacted reforms meant to protect the Indians from the most extreme abuses by *encomenderos*. But these reforms were indifferently enforced by colonial officials, who balked at angering the influential *encomendero* class. Moreover, the officials understood that the king did not expect humanitarianism to interfere with the homeward flow of his American revenues—which depended upon keeping the Indians at work on rural estates and in mines and workshops. As the Indian population declined, more village land became converted into large rural estates, known as *haciendas*, which employed the surviving natives for wages or crop shares.

During the sixteenth century, about 250,000 Spanish emigrated to the Americas. Most came from Castile and passed through the port of Seville, which monopolized Spanish trade to the Americas. Most were young, single men who took wives and concubines among the Indians, producing mixed offspring known as *mestizos*, who became especially numerous in the cities and towns. By 1700, *mestizos* outnumbered Indians in central Mexico, while imported African slaves and their offspring became the majority along the tropical coast.

In response to the mixing, the colonial authorities developed a complex new racial hierarchy known as the *castas*, which rose from the pure African and Indian at the bottom through multiple gradations of mixture to the pure Spaniard imagined at the pinnacle. The higher *castas* enjoyed superior status and greater legal privileges at the expense of the lower *castas*. The top rank of Spanish gentry dominated the *cabildos*, the councils that governed the many market towns of the new empire. Those carefully planned towns had a spacious grid of streets with the town hall and a church arranged around a central plaza. The wealthiest families dwelled near the central plaza, while the lower-caste people with darker complexions lived on the margins.

By 1550, the Spanish had created the most formidable empire in European history by conquering and colonizing in the Americas. Stretching around the Caribbean and deep into both North and South America, the empire dominated a territory more than ten times larger than Spain. The approximately twenty million Indian subjects dwarfed the seven million Spaniards at home. At the heart of the empire lay mineral-rich Mexico and Peru, whose mines exported to Spain 181 tons of gold and 16,000 tons of silver between 1500 and 1650. That wealth inspired ambitious Spaniards to imagine that other golden empires, like those of the Aztec and the Inca, must lurk just beyond reach to the north of Mexico.

In 1539, the Spanish sent northward two great *conquistador* expeditions to test the golden rumors. From Cuba, Hernando de Soto led the first to Florida and through what is now the American Southeast. From Mexico, Francisco Vázquez de Coronado marched the second expedition into and across the American Southwest to the Great Plains.

De Soto sent his 600 men on a violent rampage through the carefully cultivated and densely populated heartland of the Mississippians. Upon reaching a large village, De Soto demanded maize, women, porters, and guides. When faced with the slightest resistance, De Soto employed terror tactics to intimidate the survivors. Some Indians suffered the loss of a nose or a hand; others were thrown to the war dogs or burned alive. Finding scant gold and no silver, the *conquistadores* left a trail of corpses, mutilations, ravaged fields, emptied storehouses, and charred towns. In May 1542 De Soto sickened and died on the banks of the Mississippi. In 1543 his men gave up their expedition, building boats to descend the Mississippi and sail southwest along the Gulf Coast to Mexico. They apparently left behind epidemics, which depleted the Mississippian peoples over the course of the next generation.

Meanwhile, to the west, Coronado led an expedition of 300 Hispanic soldiers, 6 Franciscan priests, 800 Mexican Indian auxiliaries, and some 1,500 horses and pack animals. They crossed the deserts and mountains of northern Mexico to reach the Pueblo Indians of the upper Rio Grande valley. Despite their impressive adobe-brick *pueblos*, the natives lacked gold and silver, which deeply frustrated Coronado.

To get rid of their brutal and larcenous guests, the Pueblos assured them that a wealthy kingdom named Quivira lay to the distant north and east on the far side of a great, grassy plain. After weeks spent crossing the Great Plains, Coronado found only modest villages of beehive-shaped and grass-thatched lodges inhabited by Wichita Indians, who had neither gold nor silver. In frustration and fury, the Spaniards executed their native guide and marched back to the Rio Grande to resume abusing their reluctant hosts, until Coronado cut his losses and returned to northern Mexico in 1542.

Despite the expensive and destructive follies by De Soto and Coronado, the Spanish Crown felt obliged to establish northern outposts meant to protect the precious mines of Mexico by creating a buffer zone to keep away other European powers, which had begun to explore the coasts of North America.

During the 1560s, Pedro Menéndez de Avilés led the Spanish colonization of Florida. After wiping out a new settlement of French Protestants, Menéndez built a fortified town, named San Agustín (St. Augustine): the first enduring colonial town established by Europeans within the bounds of the future United States. Generating scant revenue, San Agustín proved a steady financial drain on the Spanish Crown, which paid and supplied the demoralized garrison that kept the town barely alive. Unable to attract colonists to Florida, the authorities tried to compensate by transforming Indians into Hispanics through the agency of Franciscan missionaries. During the seventeenth century, the friars established missions north of San Agustín among the Guale and Timucua, and to the west among the Apalachee of the Gulf

Coast. At the peak in 1675, forty friars ministered to 20,000 native converts who worshiped in thirty-six churches.

The governor helped by bestowing generous gifts on Indian chiefs who welcomed the priests into their villages. The Spanish also tempted the Indians with the alluring prospect of a trade to supply coveted knives, fishhooks, beads, hatchets, and blankets. Finally, the inability of traditional shamans to shield their people from the devastating new diseases induced many natives, in desperation, to hope that the newcomers offered a more powerful spiritual protection.

Conversion, however, came at a cultural cost. The priests ferreted out and burned the wooden idols cherished by the natives, banned their traditional ball game, and enforced the Christian morality that required marriage and monogamy. Converts who defied the friars suffered severe whippings, while rebellions reaped brutal and destructive reprisals by soldiers from San Agustín. And to the Indians' dismay, conversion failed to protect them from renewed waves of epidemics.

At the end of the sixteenth century, other Spaniards returned to the Rio Grande to practice a similar program of pacification by Franciscan missionaries. The priests favored the new colony as an opportunity to save Indian souls, and the Crown hoped to acquire new subjects and taxpayers who would defend the new colony as a northern buffer zone. In 1598, Don Juan de Oñate led the new colony, but his brutality provoked Indian resistance and alienated the Franciscans. By sacking Oñate, the viceroy became responsible for governing the expensive, distant, and vulnerable colony, which developed around the new town of Santa Fe.

A distant and isolated colony, New Mexico promised hardships and poverty to potential colonists. To obtain manufactured goods, including clothing and metal tools, the colonists depended upon government shipments, which arrived only once in every three or four years. Accompanied by soldiers, this caravan of ox-drawn, iron-wheeled wagons took six months to cover the 1,500-mile distance from Mexico City, much of it across harsh deserts, over steep mountains, and through the lands of hostile nomads. The high costs of overland transportation also prevented the colonists from shipping their bulky agricultural produce to market in distant Mexico. Caught in a double squeeze of high costs and small income, the New Mexicans had the lowest standard of living in North America. Never totaling more than 1,000 during the seventeenth century, the colonists remained outnumbered by the Pueblo peoples, despite the epidemics that reduced their numbers from 60,000 in 1598 to 17,000 in 1680.

By 1628 the Franciscan friars had founded fifty missions, spread throughout the Rio Grande valley and the adjoining Pecos valley. The priests had made thousands of converts, each sealed by the public sacrament of baptism, a ritual sprinkling of holy water on their heads. Christian churches obliterated and replaced the circular *kivas*—sacred structures for religious dances and ceremonies. The priests smashed, burned, or confiscated the *katsina* images sacred to the Indians, deeming them idols offensive to the true God. In addition to mastering Christianity, the Indians were supposed to dress, cook, eat, walk, and talk like Spaniards—for the friars deemed everything traditionally native to be savage and pagan.

Although the Franciscans were demanding and punitive, most Pueblo peoples decided that it was best to receive and heed them. In part, the Pueblo acted from fear of the Hispanic soldiers, who backed up the priests with their firearms, dogs, horses, whips, and gallows. Far better to ally with, than to oppose, such formidable men. Indeed, many Pueblo sought a military alliance with the Spanish against the nomadic warriors—Apache and Ute—of the nearby mountains and Great Plains. The Pueblo peoples also sought to benefit from the newcomers' metal tools and their domesticated sheep, goats, cattle, pigs, and mules, which enlarged the supply of meat and cloth, and provided power for plowing and hauling. The natives also delighted in the elaborate and novel show of the Catholic rituals—so rich in vestments, music, paintings, and sacred images. Above all, the Pueblo sought protection from the new epidemics by learning the spiritual magic of the newcomers—who suffered so much less from the diseases.

But conversions were never as complete and irreversible as the priests wanted to believe. The friars and the Pueblo had a fundamental misunderstanding—one characteristic of every missionary venture during the seventeenth century. The Franciscans erroneously believed that their native converts could entirely forsake their pagan ways, without compromise. In fact, the Pueblo combined old and new beliefs in new hybrids. While willing to add Christian beliefs and practices, as they understood them, the Pueblo continued covertly to practice their own supernatural traditions.

During the 1660s and 1670s, a prolonged drought ravaged the Pueblo crops, reducing many natives to starvation. Despite the reduced number of Pueblos and their greater poverty, the Hispanics continued to demand the same level of tribute in maize and blankets; exactions that could be tolerated in good years became intolerable in hard times. At the same time, the nomads of the Great Plains—known as Apache—increased their raids on the Pueblo, seeking to take with violence the food that they could no longer obtain in trade.

By 1675 it had become abundantly clear that the Christian God could not protect the Indians from epidemics, drought, and raiders—much less from exploitation by the Hispanics. Led by their shamans, the Pueblo peoples covertly revived their traditional ceremonies, hoping to restore the disrupted balance of their world. To suppress the revival, in 1675 the Hispanics arrested and whipped forty-seven Pueblo shamans on charges of sorcery.

One of the whipped shamans, named Popé, organized a massive rebellion, which erupted in August 1680.

The well-coordinated revolt united most of the 17,000 Pueblo people, who were joined by some Apache bands with scores to settle against the Hispanic slave-raiders. The rebels destroyed and plundered missions, farms, and ranches, procuring horses and guns. Venting their rage, the rebels took special pains to desecrate churches, smash altars, crosses, and Christian images, and to mutilate the corpses of priests. Governor Antonio de Otermín and the surviving colonists abandoned Santa Fe, fleeing south down the Rio Grande to El Paso. The rebellion killed one-fifth of the 1,000 colonists in New Mexico including twenty-one of the forty priests. In a few weeks, the Pueblo rebels had destroyed eight decades of colonial work to create Hispanic New Mexico. The Pueblo Revolt of 1680 was the greatest setback that natives ever inflicted on European expansion in North America.

But the rebellion began to falter almost as soon as it triumphed. Deprived by victory of their common enemy, the Pueblo peoples resumed their traditional feuds, falling out both within villages and between them. In addition, renewed drought brought famine and another rupture in trade with the Apache, who resumed raiding. The renewed troubles discredited Popé, who had promised that the rebellion would bring perpetual peace and prosperity. Losing influence, he died in obscurity sometime before 1690. During the 1690s, a new Hispanic governor, Diego de Vargas, led a counterattack that reclaimed New Mexico for the Spanish empire.

Bloody and destructive to the Pueblo and the Spanish, the rebellion taught both to compromise. The Pueblo peoples accepted Spanish persistence and authority, while the Hispanics practiced greater restraint. The governor abolished the *encomienda*— the extortion of labor and tribute that comprised the greatest grievance of the Pueblo. Lowering their expectations, the

4. Despite damages incurred during the Pueblo Revolt of 1680, the
Church of San Miguel in Santa Fe, New Mexico, survived. Today it is
the oldest church still standing in the United States. This photograph
shows the church as it appeared in 1873.

Franciscans wisely looked the other way when the Pueblo quietly
conducted traditional ceremonies in their *kivas*—so long as the
natives also conspicuously performed the Catholic sacramental
cycle of festivals. Finally, the Hispanics and Pueblos recognized
that they needed to ally against the nomadic warrior peoples of
the Great Plains and the Rocky Mountains. After much bloody
trial and error, the Hispanics and Pueblos had cobbled together
an unequal alliance on the northern frontier of New Spain. The
question was whether it could survive the invasion of North
America by the French and English.

In 1700, the Spanish had acquired a vast American empire of
extremes: alluring wealth and daunting power at its core in Mexico
and Peru but great poverty and vulnerability on the northern
margins. The two extremes were related, for Spanish imperial

policy favored the motherland over the colonies and the colonial core over the frontier periphery. Despairing of profiting from New Mexico or Florida, the Spanish Crown retained the northern colonies primarily as a military buffer zone meant to maximize the distance between valuable Mexico to the south and the rival European empires, which had emerged to the north and east during the previous century.

Chapter 3
New France

During the sixteenth century, the French sought a share in the American wealth that enriched and empowered the Spanish. But, as the French discovered in Florida during the 1560s, the Spanish were a powerful foe, able to destroy any hostile colony within easy reach. The French concluded that the distant northern latitudes of North America offered a safer setting for a colony. Although Canada lacked precious metals and suffered from long, cold winters, it compensated with abundant fish and the thick furs of northern mammals, then in high demand to clothe fashionable Europeans. And Canada's St. Lawrence River also offered the best access westward into the heart of the continent to trade with the Indians of the vast and fur-rich Great Lakes country. The St. Lawrence promised the French a more extensive fur trade with more northern Indian peoples than any other river system in the continent could offer.

The French trading posts began as seasonal fishing and whaling camps around the Gulf of St. Lawrence, near the mouth of the St. Lawrence River. During the sixteenth century, the sojourning mariners began to trade with Indian hunters bearing furs from beaver, fox, otter, lynx, and martin. Offering high value per volume, furs were an ideal colonial commodity that, like gold and silver, could more than pay for its transatlantic transportation.

In exchange for furs, the mariners offered European manufactured goods, especially beads, kettles, hatchets, and knives.

By enhancing the Indians' need for imported goods, trade increased their demands upon the environment. No longer hunting only to feed and clothe themselves but also to serve an external market, the northeastern natives killed more animals, especially beaver. Upon depleting their local beaver, Indians extended their hunting into the territories of their neighbors, provoking conflicts.

By providing more effective tools for killing, the new weapons increased the stakes of warfare. Indians had long conducted low-level wars of raid and counterraid, inflicting a few casualties every year. The new weapons, however, enabled the well-armed to devastate their trade-poor neighbors. In addition to taking hunting grounds, such conquests endowed victors with captive women and children to replace the hundreds lost to the new diseases. As a matter of life and death, every native people tried to attract traders and worked to keep them away from their Indian enemies.

Just as the Indians fought to control the trade, the English, French, and Dutch traders plundered and killed one another in their violent competition. To keep away rivals, the bigger trading companies built forts to control the most strategic harbors and river narrows—as Samuel de Champlain did by founding Québec in 1608. On a ridge where the St. Lawrence narrowed, Québec's cannon could block the ingress by the trading ships of rival nations and companies.

A small outpost of a few dozen men, Québec depended upon Indian goodwill to survive and prosper—unlike the military domination enjoyed by the Spanish in the heart of their silver-rich empire. The fur trade implicated traders and natives in mutual dependence. While Indians became dependent upon European metals, cloth, and alcohol, the traders became hostage to Indian demand. Needing Indians as allies and hunters, the traders could not afford them as enemies. But those alliances entangled the traders in wars against other natives.

Beginning with the Montagnais and Algonkin who lived around Québec, Champlain extended his fur-trading alliance westward into the Great Lakes country, where he drew in the Iroquoian-speaking Huron. The most tightly clustered people in the northeast, the 20,000 Huron had twenty fortified towns sustained by highly productive fields of corn, squash, and beans. They traded their surplus food to northern Indians to procure their furs, which the Huron then carried eastward in canoes to the French at Québec. To bolster that native alliance, the French established Jesuit missions among the Huron during the 1640s. After much initial reluctance, the Huron embraced the missions as new sources of supernatural power that might protect them from diseases—and that might improve their terms of trade with the French.

By framing an alliance to control the northern fur trade, the Montagnais, Algonkin, and Huron excluded the Haudenosaunee Five Nations (also known as "the Iroquois"). Dwelling to the south in what is now upstate New York (west of the Hudson, south of Lake Ontario, and east of Lake Erie), the Five Nations were, from east to west: the Mohawk, Oneida, Onondaga, Cayuga, and Seneca. As the price of business and protection, the northern nations expected the French to help them attack the Haudenosaunee.

In June 1609 Champlain and nine French soldiers joined an allied war party that ventured south to attack a Haudensaunee camp on the lake subsequently named "Champlain." Expecting a traditional Indian battle, rich in display and light in casualties, the Haudenosaunee warriors formed up in a mass, relying on wooden shields, helmets, and breastplates for protection from arrows. Springing from hiding places in the woods, Champlain

5. The title page of Gabriel Sagard's 1632 *Le grand voyage du pays des Hurons* (The Great Voyage through Huron Country) depicts Huron peoples in the top section and two Jesuit missionaries flanking the middle section.

and his soldiers stepped forward and fired, mortally wounding three Haudenosaunee chiefs, while their astonished warriors broke and fled.

This introduction of firearms revolutionized Indian warfare as the natives abandoned as useless their wooden armor and massed formations, shifting to hit-and-run raids and relying on trees for cover from gunfire. They also clamored for their own guns. As the fur trade grew more competitive, traders recognized the profits in selling what the Indians wanted most.

Unfortunately for the French and their native allies, during the 1610s the Dutch established trading posts on the Hudson River near the Haudenosaunee villages. By occupying two adjacent river systems, the French and the Dutch drew the battle lines of European commerce and empire along the preceding battle lines of native rivalry, and they raised the stakes. The Dutch traders were happy to sell guns, which cost them 6 florins each, to the eager Haudenosaunee for furs worth 120 florins in Europe.

To eliminate bloody feuds between their five nations, during the sixteenth century the Haudenosaunee had formed a confederation. Although the nations remained autonomous, they agreed to avoid attacking one another and agreed to cooperate in wars against outsiders. Indeed, internal peace refocused their warfare outward to the detriment of the many peoples living around the new confederacy. Many of their enemies were Algonkian-speakers, but the ideal targets were outsiders who spoke a related, Iroquoian language, for their cultural similarities facilitated incorporation as captives into the villages of the Five Nations.

Better armed than their foes by 1640, the Haudenosaunee attacked the Huron villages. Never before had native peoples killed on the scale and with the ferocity of the Haudenosaunee during the 1640s. By decade's end, they had burned all of the Huron villages, killing and capturing hundreds of people. During the assaults,

Jesuit priests hurriedly baptized hundreds before they too were hacked or burned to death.

During the 1650s, the Haudenosaunee next turned against the Iroquoian-speaking Erie, Petun, and Neutral nations who lived to the west around Lake Erie. Once again, the victors killed most of the defeated warriors, captured their women and children for adoption, and destroyed the villages. In 1657, a visiting French priest concluded that adopted captives had become a majority among the Haudenosaunee, whose raids also ravaged the French settlements along the St. Lawrence.

At home, French imperial officials worried that they were losing the demographic race to colonize North America. By 1663 New France had grown to just 3,000 colonists, smaller even than the 5,000 colonists planted by the tiny Netherlands along the Hudson. Worse still, by 1660 the English had 58,000 colonists in New England and the Chesapeake colonies. Impatient with Canada's slow growth, in 1663 the French Crown took over the colony from the fur-trading company.

To stimulate population growth, the Crown subsidized emigration to the struggling colony. Primarily poor, single, young men in search of work and food, most of the emigrants arrived as *engagés* obliged to serve a three-year term before they recovered their freedom. The female emigrants primarily came from an orphanage in Paris and were known as *filles du roi* (daughters of the king). In addition to paying for their passage, the Crown provided a cash marriage dowry, an alluring incentive for orphan girls, who lacked the family money expected for a marriage. The *filles du roi* promoted the formation of families, who helped to consolidate the colony. Where the *engagés* who remained single usually hastened back to France at the end of their indentures, those who married tended to stay in the colony, where most became farmers known as *habitants*.

Colonial America

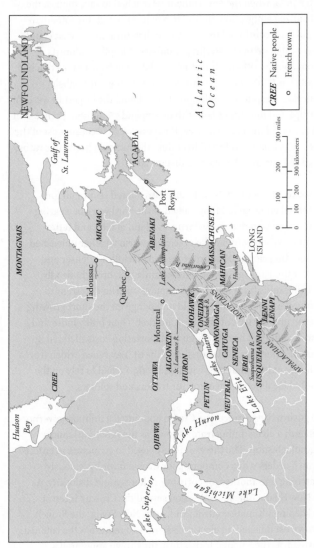

6. New France, ca. 1650.

After 1673, when the government retrenched to save money, the subsidized emigration ground to a halt. Although the Canadian population continued to grow through natural increase, it could never catch up to the swelling numbers of English colonists. From about 3,000 in 1663, the population of New France reached 15,000 in 1700—far less than the 250,000 then in English America. Despite a population of 20 million, the largest in western Europe and four times larger than England's 5 million, France sent far fewer colonists to America. Push was weak because most of the French peasants preferred to endure their known hardships rather than risk life in a strange and distant land.

Seventeenth-century New France also offered scant pull for potential emigrants. Many balked at the hard work of clearing dense forests to make new farms in a land of long and bitter winters. When winter at last receded, warm weather unleashed tormenting clouds of mosquitoes and blackflies—denser and fiercer than any in Europe. The summer also brought deadly, burning raids from the Haudenosaunee, a grim deterrent to settlers. And few farmers could prosper given the short growing season and the lack of an export market. Their bulky hides and grains could not bear the high transportation costs dictated by Canada's northern isolation far up the St. Lawrence, which froze solid for at least half the year. The *habitants* had to rely on the limited local market, feeding fur traders and soldiers.

To govern New France, the Crown appointed a military governor-general; a civil administrator known as the *intendant*; and a Catholic bishop. The three were supposed to cooperate to enforce Crown orders while competing for Crown favor by jealously watching one another for corruption, heresy, and disloyalty. As in New Spain, official contention served the Crown's interest in keeping ultimate control. And, as in New Spain, the French Crown established no elective assembly to represent the colonists. Instead, as the colonial legislature, the Crown appointed a sovereign council, consisting of five to seven leading colonists as well as the governor-general, bishop, *intendant*, and attorney general.

Most of the colonists were *habitants* who dwelled on farms along the St. Lawrence River between the two major towns, Québec and Montreal. They leased their lands from aristocratic landlords known as *seigneurs*. The roads were few and bad, so people and their goods primarily moved by horse-drawn sleighs in winter and by canoe or boat along the river in summer. Every parish featured a Catholic church, the lone faith tolerated in the colony. In the valley, some Montagnais, Huron, Abenaki, Algonkin, and Mohawk persisted in mission reserves. Their priests had learned tacitly to accept traditional customs and rituals that did not directly contradict Catholic worship. In the mission village, the Indians practiced a mix of Indian and European horticulture, but they annually dispersed for many weeks to hunt in the vast northern forest.

Farther west, beyond Montreal, and across the Great Lakes to the Mississippi, the immense hinterland hosted only a few colonists who depended upon the fur trade with the Indians. The upper-country French clustered in a few scattered settlements near forts, principally at Cahokia, Kaskaskia, and Vincennes in the Illinois country and at Detroit between Lakes Huron and Erie. In the vast Great Lakes watershed, about 2,000 French lived as a small minority on reserves among about 80,000 natives divided among many nations, mostly Algonkian-speakers.

Some of the upper-country French lived as independent fur traders. Known as *coureurs de bois*, they paddled their canoes far beyond the posts to trade with the natives at their own villages. A trader lived longer and did more business by marrying an Indian woman. Entering her kin network, he obtained the best security in the native world and the best of teachers in native ways and languages. Over the generations, these relationships produced a distinctive mixed-blood people known as the *métis*, who spoke multiple languages, lived in their own small villages, and acted as intermediaries between their French and Indian relatives.

In the upper country, the Indians and the French developed an alliance based upon mutual accommodations on what the historian Richard White has called "the middle ground." A middle ground could develop only where neither natives nor colonizers could dominate the other, where, instead, they had to deal with one another as near equals. To build an Indian alliance, the French had to arbitrate the feuds, primarily over murders. By ceremonially delivering French goods to "cover the graves" of murdered Indians, the French could unite their villages against the Haudenosaunee and the English.

The middle ground rested on creative misunderstandings. The French insisted that their king was the "father" to Indian "children." The French thus sought to command the Indians as if they were the dutiful children of a European patriarch. But the Indians did not have patriarchal families. Indeed, mothers and uncles had far more authority than did fathers. So the natives happily called the French their "fathers" in the expectation that they would behave like Indian fathers: indulgent, generous, and weak. Among Indians, a father gave much more than he received.

Armed by the French, the upper-country Indians counterattacked the Haudenosaunee, inflicting bloody defeats on their former tormentors during the 1680s and 1690s. In 1701 the beleaguered Haudenosaunee made a peace that conceded the upper country to the French and their allies. Deprived of a common enemy, the allies found new grievances with one another. In 1712 the Fox antagonized the Illinois, Miami, Ojibwa, Wyandot, Pottawatomi, and Ottawa peoples. Demanding French assistance, they threatened to destroy Detroit if denied. Unable to prevent war, the French vowed to prove their power by wiping out the Fox, whereupon their allies dropped out. Satisfied with punishing the Fox, the other Indians saw no point in allowing the French to destroy them. So the French had to make a grudging peace, while grumbling at their inability to dictate to their allies.

To expand their native alliances and contain the English colonists along the Atlantic seaboard, at the end of the seventeenth century the French established another colony to the southwest, along the Mississippi River. They named their new colony Louisiana, in honor of King Louis XIV. The capital was the port city of New Orleans near the mouth of the river. Distant from France and prone to subtropical diseases, the colony languished, attracting even fewer colonists than did Canada. In 1746 Louisiana had only 4,100 slaves, 3,300 settlers, and 600 soldiers. Nearly three-quarters of them lived on the lower Mississippi near New Orleans. Dependent on the limited trade in deerskins and plantation tobacco, the colony cost much more to administer than it yielded in revenue. The embezzling corruption of the colonial officials also drove up those administrative costs.

Lacking enough soldiers to dominate the immense hinterland, the French had to cultivate native allies, particularly the 12,000 Choctaw who lived east of the Mississippi and north of New Orleans. But the natives of the interior could be enticed by English traders, based in South Carolina, who offered better quality manufactured goods at lower prices. Put on the defensive commercially, the French compensated with gifts. During the 1730s, the Choctaw received presents worth nearly 50,000 *livres*—about twice the value of the deerskins they traded to the French. The newcomers ran their relationship with the Choctaw at a financial loss because strategic considerations took primacy over the economic in Louisiana. The French paid dearly to retain the Choctaw as their allies, to keep runaway Africans and deserting soldiers within Louisiana, and to keep the rival English traders from South Carolina out.

The French subsidized Canada and Louisiana because they needed native allies to hold the interior and contain the English colonies to the east. At great expense, the French became entangled in complicated alliances with Indians, who were struggling to adapt to the new world wrought by the colonial intrusions. Colonial empires never fulfilled the European fantasies of command and control, but they unleashed powerful forces of disease, trade, and war that, although beyond European control, disrupted native peoples.

French Louisiana drove a wedge between the northern Spanish colonies of Florida to the east and New Mexico to the west. French traders pushed up the western rivers and onto the Great Plains to arm the Indians with guns in return for pelts and slaves. The French-armed Indians obtained captives by raiding the poorly armed Pueblo peoples of New Mexico. Their Hispanic rulers resented those raids as a blow to their own security. When facing east, the French opposed the English slave trade based in Carolina, but in facing west, the French encouraged their Great Plains clients to prey on the Pueblo of New Mexico.

During the eighteenth century, an Indian trade became the key to expanding a North American empire. Although commercially weaker than the British of Carolina, the French of Louisiana had the edge as Indian traders over the Spanish of New Mexico. Compared to the French, the workshops in Spain were less productive, Spanish shipping was more expensive, and Spanish regulations compounded the cost of consumer goods. Plus, the Spanish balked at trading guns to Indians.

Although they derived new power from the French trade, the Indians of the Great Plains did not, in fact, act as French pawns. In raiding the Hispanics and the Pueblo, the Plains Indians aggressively pursued their own interests—with French weapons. They sought revenge for Hispanic slave-raiding—as well as horses and captives to pay for more French goods.

For centuries, the vast, grassy, and windy region had belonged to many far-flung tribes of two sorts. On the western half of the plains, nomadic bands lived in mobile camps of bison-hide tents. They specialized in hunting the bison (or "buffalos"), a hard and dangerous life for people without horses, as the bison were large, powerful animals that moved in huge herds. On the eastern half of the plains, the river valleys hosted permanent and substantial villages of up to 2,000 people who lived in lodges burrowed into the earth. They grew crops in alluvial fields and occasionally ventured out onto the surrounding plains to hunt buffalo. The nomads were Athapaskan-speakers later known as Apaches, while the earth-lodge villagers were either Caddoan-speakers (including the Arikara, Caddo, Pawnee, and Wichita) or Siouan-speakers (including the Hidatsa, Kansa, Mandan, Omaha, Osage, and Ponca).

Although every village was independent, people who spoke a common language and who intermarried and practiced similar ceremonies ordinarily cooperated in hunting and war. In particular, as the nomadic bands shifted eastward they came into conflict with the villagers. But some nomads and some earth-lodge dwellers reduced conflict by engaging in a trade of buffalo meat for corn, squash, and beans.

We now imagine that the mounted warrior and buffalo hunter was the typical Indian and the defender of a timeless way of life that predated the European invasion of America. In fact, the Great Plains Indians had no horses until the end of the seventeenth century. They then procured them by raiding the Spanish ranches of New Mexico, especially after the Pueblo revolt of 1680 had disrupted Hispanic rule. From Apache and Kiowa middlemen, the horses gradually spread northward through trade and theft to become abundant among the native peoples of the Northern Plains by 1750.

The horses enriched the lives of people who lived by buffalo hunting on the Great Plains. On horseback, men could cover far more ground in much less time, and they could see farther, finding buffalo herds more easily and quickly. Faster and nimbler than the buffalo, the horses enabled mounted men armed with bows to maneuver and attack with deadly rapidity. By killing more buffalo, the Great Plains peoples became better fed, clothed, and housed. Compared to a dog, a horse could haul loads four times larger, enabling the Indians to acquire and transport more possessions over longer distances.

But the rich new possibilities of the mounted life on the Great Plains attracted a growing array of new competitors. From the Rocky Mountains to the west emigrated the Kiowa, a Uto-Aztecan people, and the Comanche, a Shoshonean-speaking people. From the east in the upper Mississippi valley came more Siouan-speakers, particularly the Lakota (or Dakota) tribes, and Algonkian-speaking Blackfoot, Arapaho, and Cheyenne. In sum, most of the Indian peoples we now associate with the Great Plains were newcomers who arrived during the eighteenth century.

Because the villagers defended the river bottoms that could sustain horticulture, most of the newcomers became nomads on the vast grasslands. The growing competition for the buffalo herds led to widespread wars between men on horseback. In addition to promoting the hunting of buffalo, the horses facilitated the killing of people—as did the new guns obtained from French traders. The swirling wars pitted nomads against nomads as well as nomads against villagers in shifting patterns of alliances and trade.

The supplies of horses and guns flowed unevenly, favoring some native peoples at the expense of others. If a better-mounted and better-armed people captured a territory rich with buffalo, their advantages became compounded to the detriment of their rivals. By stealing from the weak, the strong grew still stronger in people, horses, and firearms at the expense of the losers. Driven out by the victors, the defeated could survive only by fleeing in search of a new territory, where they might prey upon some even weaker people.

On the Southern Plains, the Comanche became the big winners by taking women, horses, buffalo, and land from the Apache. The victors compounded their advantages by trading captives and hides to the French for more guns—which facilitated yet more raids on the Apache. By 1800 the Comanche numbered about 20,000, twice as many as all other native peoples on the Southern Plains. Reeling from Comanche raids, Apache refugees fled westward across the Rio Grande into New Mexico, where they raided the Hispanics and Pueblo, taking horses, sheep, cattle, and captives.

The French trade had ruined the Spanish monopoly in guns that had been critical to their domination in New Mexico. Lashing back in 1720, the governor of New Mexico sent a mixed force of Hispanic soldiers and Pueblo allies across the Great Plains to attack the Pawnee and their French traders. There they fell into a Pawnee ambush, which routed the Hispanics, killing their commander, Pedro de Villasur, in an embarrassing and crushing setback for New Mexico.

Overmatched in a trade war for Indian favor, the Spanish tried instead to expand their traditional combination of Franciscan missions and military *presidios* eastward into the contested border zone. Founded during the 1710s, Hispanic Texas consisted of the town of San Antonio, ten missions, and 250 soldiers in four scattered *presidios* in 1722. Thereafter the colony stagnated as few Hispanics moved to a colony even more distant, dangerous, and impoverished than New Mexico. The colonists sustained a hardscrabble existence by supplying their *presidios* with provisions, by driving longhorn cattle south for sale to the silver miners of Mexico, and by smuggling with French Louisiana, which defeated the official purpose of founding Texas. The Spanish had compounded their exposed frontier by adding a second cluster of weak and unprofitable settlements in Texas.

Indeed, Texas increased the Hispanic vulnerability to the warriors of the Great Plains. Fleeing from the Comanche, some Apache sought refuge at a new mission and presidio founded in 1757 on the San Saba River, north of San Antonio; thereby the Hispanics became a party to the Apache conflict with the Comanche and their Wichita allies. In 1758 hundreds of mounted Comanche and Wichita warriors destroyed the San Saba mission, killing

49

the Hispanics, including two priests. In 1759 the Spanish and their Apache allies counterattacked by sending raiders north to the Red River to attack a stockaded Wichita village, which flew a provocative French flag given by Louisiana officials. Once again, the Spanish suffered a bloody and humiliating defeat at the hands of well-armed Indians.

Formerly dominant over Indians without guns and horses, the Hispanics saw that the tables had turned as the Great Plains tribes became armed and mounted—and capable of destroying colonial outposts like San Saba. The European invasion of North America initiated sweeping changes that transformed native peoples, but on the Great Plains those changes had escaped from the control of the colonizers and especially of the Hispanics. The French system of alliances based on trade was trumping the older Spanish reliance on the combination of missions and *presidios* to pin down and dominate native peoples.

Chapter 4
Chesapeake colonies

During the sixteenth century, Spanish and French colonizers bypassed the long coast north of Florida and south of Acadia (Nova Scotia). They deemed that temperate region too cool for tropical crops but too warm for the best furs. Consequently, the mid-Atlantic seaboard remained open to colonization by the English, who called that entire coast "Virginia" to honor their queen, Elizabeth I, a supposed virgin. To lead the settlement of Virginia, she licensed ambitious courtiers from the southwestern counties of England. Known as "the West Country men," they looked westward toward Ireland and beyond for opportunities. By founding colonies, they hoped to weaken the empire of their great enemy, Catholic Spain.

The West Country promoters also promised to resolve England's growing problems with poverty, vagrancy, and crime. During the later sixteenth century, the English economy stagnated while the population grew. Landlords displaced thousands of rural peasants by enclosing their lands within fences and substituting herds of sheep tended by hired laborers. In the long term, enclosure increased agricultural productivity and wealth of the already rich. In the short term, however, enclosure rendered superfluous, homeless, and miserable thousands of peasants and laborers. They headed to the towns where, when unable to find work, they became beggars. As a last resort, they stole, which sent many to the gallows, for theft was a capital crime. The growing numbers of the poor also depressed the wages that employers had to pay. Meanwhile, inflation added to the squeeze on real wages, which fell to half of their 1500 level by 1650, depressing the already bleak living conditions of the poor.

Appealing to the alarm of propertied Englishmen, the West Country promoters urged the export of sturdy beggars to a new colony in Virginia, where the poor could be put to work raising commodities for transport to England. By producing commodities that could not be raised at home, colonial plantations could improve England's balance of trade with other nations. In sum, the promoters offered a neat package that would control and employ the poor while generating new wealth and power for the realm.

The West Country promoters insisted that the Indians would regard the English as kinder and gentler colonizers than the Spanish. Invoking the so-called Black Legend that the Spanish were uniquely brutal colonizers, the promoters insisted that the Indians would welcome the English as liberators. But the English had been far from gentle liberators in their recent conquest of Ireland. Indeed, that brutal conquest served as their school for overseas empire, the English equivalent of the Spanish invasion of the Canaries.

In 1585 Sir Walter Ralegh, a West Country promoter, planted the first English colony at Roanoke, a small, sandy island on the North Carolina coast. When the local Indians refused to provide food, the colonists massacred the local chiefs. But that yielded no more food, so the first set of colonists sailed home. Ralegh's second set arrived but soon vanished, apparently into the country where the Indians either killed or assimilated them.

In 1607 the English tried again, this time to the north at Chesapeake Bay, which offered better harbors, navigable rivers, and a more fertile land. About two hundred miles long and twenty miles wide, the bay was a complex system of waterways, an environmental meeting place of tidewater estuaries and freshwater rivers, which offered ready navigation about 100 miles upstream until interrupted by waterfalls, where the coastal plain gave way to the rolling hills of the Piedmont.

The broad coastal plain sustained about 24,000 Indians divided into thirty tribes but united by an Algonkian language and the rule of a paramount chief named Powhatan. The natives practiced a mix of horticulture, fishing, hunting, and gathering. Living close to the bone, the Indians had precious little surplus to tide them over in case of some unanticipated shortfall like an infestation of worms in the corn or the arrival of hungry and well-armed colonists.

Powerfully built, savvy, and dignified, Powhatan led the most powerful chiefdom that the English found along the Atlantic seaboard. Unlike a nation-state, which relied upon a bureaucracy and army to maintain obedience and collect taxes, a paramount chiefdom was an elaborate kinship network that gathered and redistributed tribute. He took one hundred wives from subordinated chiefdoms to produce numerous sons to govern their villages in the next generation. Powhatan left the subordinate chiefs alone so long as they paid their tribute in wives, maize, and deerskins, and so long as they joined his war parties sent against the Siouan-speaking Monacans and Mannahoacs of the Piedmont. The natives waged a war of quick raids meant to kill a few warriors, take some captives, and humiliate a rival—before beating a hasty retreat homeward to celebrate. Lacking professional armies, the Indians could not sustain the protracted and long-distance campaigns of conquest like those of the English in Ireland.

Rather than crush the newcomers from England, Powhatan sought to turn them to his advantage. He hoped to contain them, subject to his power as subordinate allies to help fight the Monacans and Mannahoacs. Above all, Powhatan wanted to secure through trade or tribute their metals, including weapons. Unable to predict the future, the Algonkians did not know that the initial few colonists were the opening wedge for thousands to follow, bent upon transforming the land and destroying the Indian world.

For their part, the ethnocentric English were poorly prepared to understand and accept a culture so different from their own. Because the English worshiped a single omnipotent God, they disdained the native pantheism as paganism, at best, and devil-worship, at worst. Coming from a culture that coveted private property and demanded heavy labor, the colonial leaders considered the Indians lazy and backward. Those leaders also feared that their own laborers so hated civilized discipline that they would try to run away to live in greater ease with the Indians. The colonizers meant to subordinate the Indians, lest the lower-sort colonists turn Indian and thus against the colony.

Unlike the Spanish in Florida and the French in Canada, the English sent no missionaries to convert the Indians of Virginia. Instead, the English meant first to absorb the Indians as economic subordinates, who could then be taught Protestant Christianity at the regular church services of the colonists. Ignoring the Indian villages and fields, the English insisted that Virginia was a wilderness that their God required them to take and improve into productive farmland. Indians who resisted could expect to be treated like wild and dangerous beasts. The English sense of superiority remained impervious to their own follies as colonists in a land long mastered by the Indians.

After Ralegh and the other West Country men lost favor at the royal court, leadership over the colonial project fell to the Virginia Company, a cartel of London merchants with a charter from the Crown. They sent three vessels to the Chesapeake, arriving there in April 1607. Seeking security from Spanish discovery and attack, the colonists sailed up the James River about sixty miles to establish Jamestown beside a swamp on the north bank. They named both river and town to flatter their new king, James I. For further protection, the colonists surrounded their wooden huts with a triangular stockade mounted with cannon.

The swampy location proved deadly, for it bred millions of mosquitoes, carriers of malaria. The colonists also suffered salt poisoning from the brackish water of their wells. Those who lived were often too weak and apathetic to work, so they starved. Of the initial 104, nine months later only 38 lived. Between 1607 and 1622 the Virginia Company transported another 10,000 people to the colony, but only 20 percent were still alive there in 1622.

Even when healthy, many early colonists refused to work diligently at raising crops to feed themselves, for they preferred to search for gold and to extort corn from the Indians. After all, the promoters had insisted that the natives would welcome the English with generosity and submission. And what was the purpose of being civilized Christians with superior arms and armor if not to command the weaker, heathen peoples of new lands? The colonists did not understand that the local Indians had scant surplus to spare.

And to Powhatan's dismay, the colonists refused to trade the weapons that he so coveted. The Indians lashed back, killing seventeen intruders, stuffing their dead mouths with corn as a sign of contempt. The colonists responded with escalating violence, burning villages and massacring their men, women, and children. The raiders also captured some fellow colonists who had run away to the Indians to escape the hunger, hardships, and brutality of their domineering leaders. The governor made examples by burning them at the stake or breaking their backs slowly on the wheel.

The conflict abated in 1613 when the colonists captured Powhatan's favorite daughter, Pocahontas. Held in Jamestown and indoctrinated by the English, she accepted Christian conversion, took the name Rebecca, and married John Rolfe in 1614. Weary of war, Powhatan made peace with the colonists. In 1617 Pocahontas visited England, where she promptly died of disease.

Powhatan expired a year later, and power passed to his brother Opechancanough.

The colony also benefited from John Rolfe's development of tobacco as a cash crop that could bear the high cost of transportation to market in England. Consumers would pay premium prices to satisfy their craving for the addictive nicotine. Because tobacco plants prefer a long, hot, and humid growing season, the crop thrived in Virginia but not in England, giving the colonial farmers a comparative advantage. Virginia's tobacco production swelled from 200,000 pounds in 1624 to 3,000,000 pounds in 1638. Drawn to Virginia by tobacco's profits, the colonial population surged from only 350 in 1616 to 13,000 by 1650. As tobacco cultivation expanded and the population grew, the planters needed more land, which they took from the Indians.

This expansion provoked renewed war. On March 22, 1622, Opechancanough led a well-coordinated surprise attack, which destroyed the out-lying plantations, killing 347 men, women, and children. The survivors rallied at Jamestown and a few other fortified settlements, while the natives killed livestock and burned plantations. The Virginians developed the strategy, practiced in subsequent colonial wars, of waiting until just before corn harvest to attack and destroy the native villages and their crops, consigning the survivors to a winter and spring of starvation. In 1632 Opechancanough accepted a bitter peace, granting massive land concessions. Twelve years later, he staged a second and even deadlier surprise attack, killing more than 400 colonists. But the colonists then destroyed most of the Indian towns along the rivers, dispersing the survivors into the hinterland. Captured by the English, Opechancanough was shot dead in a Jamestown street, terminating the paramount chiefdom built by Powhatan. Disease and war reduced the Virginia Algonkians from 24,000 in 1607 to only 2,000 by 1669.

While the Indians dwindled on the coastal plain, the colonial numbers continued to surge from 13,000 in 1650 to 41,000 in

MATOAKA ALS REBECCA FILIA POTENTISS : PRINC : POWHATANI IMP : VIRGINIÆ.

Ætatis suæ 21. A. 1616

Matoaks als Rebecka daughter to the mighty Prince Powhatan Emperour of Attanoughkomouck als virginia converted and baptized in the Christian faith, and wife to the wor⁰ Mr. Joh. Rolff.

S. Pass: sculp: Compton Holland excud

7. Pocahontas's fashionable clothing indicates the potential for the "civilization" of the New World envisioned by Europeans. This engraving, the only known portrait of its subject from life, was commissioned by the Virginia Company from the Dutch artist Simon Van de Passe during Pocahontas's stay in London from 1616 until her untimely death in 1617.

1670. By the end of the 1660s, the colonists annually shipped 10 million pounds of tobacco to England—up from 3 million pounds in 1638. But the boom failed to save the teetering Virginia Company from Crown foreclosure in 1624. Virginia became the first royal colony in the new English empire.

In 1632 the Crown set aside the land at the northern head of Chesapeake Bay as a second colony, named "Maryland" after the queen of the new monarch, Charles I (son of James). The king gave the new colony to a political ally, Cecilius Calvert, the second Lord Baltimore, to own and govern as a "proprietary colony." He promised refuge for his fellow Roman Catholics, who were harassed in England by the Protestant majority. To set a model for toleration, Baltimore's colony also welcomed Protestants, who became the majority. By attracting experienced colonists from Virginia, Maryland benefited from their expertise. With fewer and shorter growing pains, Maryland rapidly prospered as a tobacco colony.

In theory, the Chesapeake colonists lived in a political hierarchy with four tiers. At the top was the distant king, governing the realm in collaboration with Parliament. Closer to home, the colonist answered to the provincial government: the governor, council, and assembly meeting in Jamestown or in St. Mary's City in Maryland. The county court and parish vestry followed next down the political ladder and closer to the common colonist. The fourth and most intimate tier of government was the family household, which the English called a "little commonwealth." The political culture insisted that the health and survival of the county, colony, and realm all depended upon the order, morality, and allegiance maintained in the many little commonwealths.

Every little commonwealth had a petty monarch, ordinarily a married man, more rarely a widow. Indeed, widows were few and their status brief in colonies where women were in such short supply and in such great demand for remarriage. The husband also supervised and disciplined his dependents: wife, children, and servants. By the law of "coverture," married women had neither legal nor political existence but depended upon their husbands to represent the household to the outside society. By law only the head of the household could own land and make contracts, and only male heads could vote, serve on juries, or hold political office.

Because of the Chesapeake's skewed sex ratio, many men never found the wives needed to form households and families. In 1625, men comprised 74 percent of Virginia's population; only 10 percent were women, and the remaining 16 percent were children. The gender gap later diminished, but throughout the seventeenth century, men greatly outnumbered women in the Chesapeake. The prevalence of single men deprived the Chesapeake colonies of a stable foundation of little commonwealths, increasing the social volatility.

During the seventeenth century, only a quarter of the Chesapeake immigrants arrived as free men and women who could afford to pay their own passage and immediately obtain land. The free arrivals ranged from skilled artisans, farmers, and petty traders to wealthy merchants and gentlemen. Endowed with an immense head start in the race for wealth and political influence, the free emigrants became the councilors, assemblymen, and justices of the colonial government.

Three-quarters of the immigrants arrived as indentured servants. Too poor to afford the £6 cost of a transatlantic passage, the servants mortgaged four to seven years of their lives to a ship captain or merchant, who carried them to the Chesapeake for sale to tobacco planters. Unpaid during their terms, the servants received basic food, clothing, and shelter—generally just enough to keep them alive and working. At the conclusion of a term, the master was supposed to endow his servant with "freedom dues"—a new set of clothes, tools, and food. During the first half of the seventeenth century, Virginia and Maryland also provided each "freedman" with fifty acres of land. Given that a sturdy beggar could never obtain land in England, the colony offered an opportunity unavailable at home. Of course, that opportunity required men and women to gamble their lives in a dangerous land of hard work and many diseases. Most lost their gamble, dying before their terms expired. Despite importing 15,000 indentured servants between 1625 and 1640, Virginia's population increased by only 7,000.

At mid-century, the Chesapeake became a bit healthier, and many more servants lived long enough to claim their freedom and farms. In 1648 a Virginian marveled that only one in nine immigrants died during their first year, compared to five of six during the preceding generation. In part, health improved as many new plantations expanded upstream into locales with fresh, running streams, in contrast to the stagnant lowlands, which favored malaria, dysentery, and typhoid fever. In addition, over time a growing proportion of the population became "seasoned" by surviving bouts with the local diseases. The seasoned acquired a higher level of immunity, which they passed on to their offspring.

The mid-century age of opportunity for common planters was brief, for social mobility quickly diminished after 1665. The swelling number of growers glutted the English market with tobacco. With one pence per pound the minimum tobacco price for breaking even, planters faced ruin during the late 1660s and early 1670s, when the price plummeted to half a pence per pound. They also struggled to pay the heavy taxes demanded by the corrupt administration of Sir William Berkeley, the royal governor of Virginia. New freedmen failed to find good land because the wealthier planters had consolidated large plantations along the rivers. The freedmen had to accept tenancy or move to the frontier, where they provoked new conflicts with the Indians.

In 1675 war erupted between the settlers on the Potomac and the Susquehannocks, an Iroquoian-speaking people who dwelled to their north. The settlers demanded permission from the governor to exterminate all the natives on the frontier, no matter how peaceable. Used to governing with a high hand, Berkeley refused to concede his command over Indian policy to frontier leaders. He preferred a defensive strategy that built an expensive system of new forts, which outraged settlers as a waste of money and which added to their taxes while further enriching the governor and his cronies with construction contracts.

The disgruntled Virginians turned to an ambitious and charismatic newcomer, a twenty-nine-year-old gentleman named Nathaniel Bacon. To popular acclaim, Bacon led indiscriminate attacks on the Indians in open defiance of the governor. Because friendly Algonkians were closer and easier to catch, they died in greater numbers than did the more elusive Susquehannocks. Declared a traitor by Berkeley in early 1676, Bacon marched his armed followers to Jamestown to attack the governor.

In part, "Bacon's Rebellion" represented a division within the planter elite, a split between a cabal allied with the royal governor and a rival set of ambitious but frustrated planters who resented their relative lack of patronage from Berkeley. But in order to prevail, the rebel leaders needed to recruit armed support among the common people by pledging redress for their grievances. Bacon promised immediate freedom to servants who deserted Berkeley's supporters to join the rebellion. He also encouraged the poor to plunder the plantations of Berkeley's friends, and Bacon implied that he would lower taxes and provide better lands to the freedmen.

In September 1676, Bacon's men drove the governor and his supporters out of Jamestown and across Chesapeake Bay to refuge on the Eastern Shore. To discourage their return, Bacon burned Jamestown to the ground. A month later, however, Bacon suddenly died of dysentery, leaving his movement leaderless and divided. Returning to the Western Shore, Berkeley routed the rebels and then hung twenty-three of them. The violence disturbed the king, who blamed Berkeley for disrupting the tobacco trade that generated so much Crown revenue. The king sent a small army to restore order and to sack Berkeley, who returned to England in disgrace.

In Bacon's Rebellion and the Crown intervention, the great planters received a double scare; internal rebellion had been bad enough, but external interference was worse. Fearing a future assertion of Crown power, the great planters felt compelled to appease the common planters. The assembly dramatically reduced the poll tax, the most burdensome levy borne by the poor planter. At the turn of the century, cross-class relations also improved as European demand increased the price of tobacco and, thus, the income of all planters. The assemblymen also embraced Bacon's policy of aggressive westward expansion to provide farms for the growing population of common planters. To maintain their political ascendancy, the great planters needed to lead, rather than oppose, wars against the Indians. Frontier wars led poor whites to see a better future in the dispossession of Indians rather than in rebellion against their planter elite.

Relations between the common whites and the great planters also improved as the numbers of indentured servants dwindled. English emigration to the Chesapeake declined from 18,000 during the 1660s to 13,000 during the 1680s. Economic growth in England pushed up real wages at the same time that bad economic news from the Chesapeake discouraged potential emigrants. Better able to feed, clothe, and house themselves in England, more poor folk decided to stay home. During the 1680s and 1690s, those who did emigrate preferred other, newer colonies—Jamaica, Carolina, and Pennsylvania—that offered the sort of frontier opportunities that had dissipated in the Chesapeake.

As English servants became scarcer and more expensive, African slaves became a better investment for the Chesapeake planters.

It also helped that slave traders began to visit the Chesapeake in swelling numbers, increasing the supply to meet the growing demand. The slave numbers surged from a mere 300 in 1650 to 13,000 by 1700, when Africans comprised 13 percent of the Chesapeake population. During the early eighteenth century, their numbers and proportion continued to grow, reaching 150,000 people (40 percent of the total) by 1750.

The planters shifted from servants to slaves for economic reasons, but that change incidentally improved their security against another rebellion by angry freedmen. During the 1670s, a host of new freedmen had entered a society of diminishing opportunity. Frustrated and armed, they had rebelled in 1676. Thereafter, fewer servants meant fewer new freedmen who might become frustrated and rebel. Bacon's Rebellion did not cause the switch from servants to slaves, but that shift did diminish the motives for poor white rebellion. Instead, the great planters increasingly dreaded an uprising by their slaves. To intimidate and guard the slaves, the masters needed a militia drawn from the common farmers. No longer a threat to the social order, the common whites instead defended it against slave rebellion.

Early in the century Chesapeake slavery had been relatively amorphous and fluid. Masters had permitted slaves to acquire and manage their own livestock and small garden plots of corn and tobacco. Dozens made enough money to buy their freedom and small farms. The black freedmen and women could move as they pleased, baptize their children, procure firearms, testify in court, buy and sell property, marry white people, and even vote.

Late in the century, as slaves became numerous and alarming, the Chesapeake masters and their assemblymen defined slavery more strictly. Slaves had to work longer days under stricter supervision than had servants. After tending tobacco and corn all day, they often labored late into the night pounding corn by hand. The planters also afforded the Africans even less food, poorer housing, and less medical attention than servants had received. Masters insisted that only pain and fear could motivate slaves, for unlike servants, slaves could not be punished with added years of service. Instead, they had to feel the lash. The authorities held no master liable for the death of his slave from excessive punishment. The planters rationalized their increased brutality by deriding the Africans as stupid brutes. By pretending to the stubborn stupidity projected upon them, some slaves slyly frustrated their masters, but it was always a dangerous contest.

New laws restricted the movement and trading by slaves. None could leave a plantation without a written pass from the master. Militia squads patrolled the roads to demand passes, to inspect slave quarters for weapons, and to break up gatherings of visiting blacks. After 1691 no Virginia planter could free slaves unless he paid for their transportation beyond the colony. Free blacks lost the right to bear arms, hold office, vote, or employ white servants. Despite their poverty, free blacks had to pay higher taxes, and the courts inflicted stricter penalties on free blacks than whites when convicted for the same crimes.

New laws also promoted racial solidarity by all whites across class lines. In 1680 Virginia prescribed thirty lashes on the bare back of any black slave who threatened or struck any white person, which invited poor whites to bully slaves with impunity, creating a common sense of white mastery over all blacks. The assembly also forbade interracial marriage and criminalized interracial sex where the woman was white. Of course, the assembly passed in silence over the far more numerous cases where white masters procreated with enslaved women. Raping a slave was not a crime but marrying her was.

As the great planters created a racial system of slavery, the common and the great planters both found a new, shared identity that held every white man superior to every black. A dark skin became synonymous with slavery, just as freedom became equated with whiteness. Meanwhile, the planter elite continued to concentrate most property and real power in their own hands, obliging young and ambitious commoners to move westward to build farms on the frontier.

After an immense cost in lives—native and colonist—the English had secured a lucrative, dynamic, and expansive base on the North American continent. Their once tenuous beachhead had become two thriving provinces and a dynamo for further expansion. As the West Country promoters had hoped, Virginia and Maryland consumed English manufactures and produced an agricultural staple that replaced an import, improving England's balance of trade. And, as the promoters had predicted, the Chesapeake absorbed thousands of poor laborers considered superfluous and dangerous in England. But the West Country promoters could not have predicted that peace between the Virginia commoners and the gentry would be purchased by enslaving thousands of Africans. Colonial Virginians developed the American interdependence of elite rule, popular politics, and white racial supremacy. That distinctive combination increasingly distinguished English America from the mother country and from the colonies of other empires.

Chapter 5
New England

During the early seventeenth century, the English founded a second set of colonies in New England, to the north of the Chesapeake. New England attracted a different sort of colonist, primarily people of "middling" prosperity who espoused Puritanism, a more demanding form of Protestantism than the Anglicanism practiced in the Chesapeake. Puritans came from all ranks of English society, including a few aristocrats, but most were small-property owners: farmers, shopkeepers, and skilled artisans with a leg up on the impoverished and underemployed half of the English population. Offering a strict code of personal discipline and morality, Puritanism helped thousands of ordinary people cope with the economic and social turmoil of England. Puritans insisted that men honored God by working hard in their occupation—which they deemed a "calling" bestowed by God.

Radical Protestants, the Puritans insisted that the monarchs of England had failed sufficiently to reform the Anglican Church, which seemed still tainted by Roman Catholic doctrines, ceremonies, and the hierarchy of bishops and archbishops, with the king substituting for the pope at the top. Most English Puritans remained within the Anglican Church, seeking to capture and reform it, while the most radical became "Separatists" who withdrew into their own independent congregations. Lacking any larger authority to enforce orthodoxy, the autonomous Separatist congregations splintered in their beliefs and practices, forming dozens of distinct sects.

By moral living, devout prayer, reading the Bible, and heeding sermons, the hopeful Puritan prepared for the possibility of God's saving grace. But not even the most devout could claim conversion and salvation as a right and a certainty, for God alone determined. He saved selectively and arbitrarily, rather than universally or as a reward for good behavior. In this insistence upon God's complete power over grace and salvation, the Puritans adhered to the Calvinist doctrines of the Swiss theologian John Calvin. Despite their apparently fatalistic belief, Puritans were incorrigible doers, ever preaching, seeking, and proposing radical schemes for improving society and disciplining the immoral and indolent. They implicitly believed that godly doing attested to probable salvation, although no one could be certain.

Puritans blamed immorality, indolence, and indulgent authorities for the social and economic troubles of the realm. They insisted that England could be cleansed of poverty and crime if godly men and women united to take charge of their churches and governments, introducing moral rigor to both. This zeal dismayed most English people, who preferred Anglicanism and the traditional culture characterized by church ales, Sunday diversions, ceremonial services, inclusive churches, and deference to the monarch. The Puritan rigor also alarmed the kings, who wanted a united and quiet realm of unquestioning loyalty. They saw subversive potential in the Puritans' insistence on the spiritual equality of all godly men and on their superiority to all ungodly men, including most of the king's bishops. During the late 1620s, Archbishop William Laud sought to purge Puritan ministers from the Anglican Church and to punish any who published their ideas.

Most Puritans stuck it out in England, but some left for "New England," a name applied to the northern reaches of the Atlantic seaboard. In 1620 the first emigrants consisted of 102 Puritan Separatists, subsequently called "the Pilgrims," who crossed the Atlantic in the *Mayflower* to found the town of Plymouth on the south shore of Massachusetts Bay. Beneficiaries of an epidemic that had recently devastated the coastal Indians, the Plymouth colonists occupied an abandoned village with conveniently cleared fields.

In 1630 a much larger emigration of orthodox Puritans— subsequently called "the Great Migration"—began under the leadership of John Winthrop. A lawyer and member of the gentry, Winthrop represented a syndicate of wealthy Puritans who had obtained a royal charter as the Massachusetts Bay Company. By moving to New England, they converted their commercial charter into a self-governing colony 3,000 miles away from bishops and king. Beginning with a settlement named Boston, Winthrop's Puritans established the Massachusetts Bay Colony on the coast north of Plymouth. They founded a virtually independent republic, where the Puritan men elected their governor, deputy governor, and legislature. During the 1630s, "the Great Migration" brought about 14,000 colonists to New England. But that surge proved brief, declining to a trickle after 1640. Thereafter, population growth depended primarily on natural increase by those who had emigrated during the 1630s.

By colonial standards, New England attracted an unusual set of emigrants, the sort of skilled and prosperous people who ordinarily stayed at home rather than risk the rigors of a transatlantic crossing and the hazards of colonial life. Most seventeenth-century emigrants to the other colonies were poor, young, single men, lacking good prospects in the mother country. In sharp contrast, indentured servants comprised less than one-fifth of the New England emigrants, for most could pay their own way and emigrated as family groups. The immigrants also enjoyed a more even balance between the sexes: six males for every four females compared to four men for every woman in the Chesapeake.

Greater balance encouraged a more stable society and a faster population growth.

They also came to a healthier land. In contrast to the long, hot, and humid summers and low landscape of the Chesapeake tidewater, New England was a northern and hilly country with a short growing season and fast-running rivers and streams. Those conditions discouraged the spread of the malaria that so afflicted southern colonists. In New England, adults could expect to live to about seventy, whereas in the Chesapeake few survived beyond fifty.

This healthier and more gender-balanced population grew rapidly through natural increase—in contrast to the Chesapeake and West Indies where growth depended on continued human imports. During the seventeenth century, New England received only 21,000 emigrants—a fraction of the 120,000 transported to the Chesapeake and of the 190,000 who colonized the West Indies. Yet in 1700 New England's colonial population of 91,000 exceeded the 85,000 in the Chesapeake and the 33,000 resident in the West Indies. Despite attracting the fewest emigrants, healthy New England became the most populous region in English America.

Pushing northeast from Boston, some Puritans settled along the coasts of New Hampshire and Maine, where they mingled uneasily with fishing folk, nominal Anglicans who came from the English West Country. Southeastern New England became a haven for radical Separatists who settled around Narragansett Bay in towns that eventually formed the colony of Rhode Island. At the other religious extreme, some especially conservative Puritans bolted from Massachusetts to found the colonies of Connecticut and New Haven along the Connecticut River and Long Island Sound.

The New England colonies granted lands to men who banded together as a corporate group to found a town, which distributed the lands. This town system contrasted with the Chesapeake colonies, where the wealthy and well-connected obtained very large tracts along the rivers, which dispersed settlement. New England's more compact settlement pattern by towns favored public schools, mutual supervision of morality, and a nearby and well-attended local church. Because the towns distributed their lands in a relatively egalitarian fashion, most families held between 100 and 200 acres—sufficient for a farm but not for a plantation.

The northern climate, short growing season, and rough, stony land precluded raising the colonial staples in greatest European demand: tobacco and sugar. Instead, the New English farmers raised a mix of wheat, rye, corn, potatoes, beans, and garden plants. They also tended a few livestock, a mix of oxen, cows, horses, sheep, and pigs. None could be profitably shipped for sale in England, where a similar climate permitted the same crops and animals. The farm families consumed most of their own produce and traded their small surpluses for the goods and services of local artisans, principally carpenters, blacksmiths, and shoemakers.

Unable to afford servants or slaves, most of the New Englanders instead relied upon the family labor of their sons and daughters. In 1700 less than 2 percent of New England's inhabitants were slaves, compared to 13 percent for Virginia and 78 percent for the English West Indies. Compared to the Chesapeake or West Indies colonies, social gradations were subtle among the New English, for most belonged to the "middling sort." The largest seaports—Boston, Salem, and Newport—did host a wealthy elite of merchants, lawyers, and land speculators, but they enjoyed less power than did the great planters of the South.

To procure an export commodity, the New English developed a fleet of fishing boats, which sought cod on the nearby Georges Bank and on the larger Grand Banks near Newfoundland. Their catch grew from 600,000 pounds of fish in 1641 to 6 million pounds in 1675. Along with some farm produce and much lumber, the seaport merchants shipped the fish to the West Indies to feed the slaves of the sugar plantations. By the 1690s more than 70 percent of New England's exports went to the West Indies.

New England's fisheries and the carrying trade stimulated shipbuilding. Blessed with an abundant supply of cheap and good timber, New England's shipbuilders could produce ships at half the cost of London shipyards. Between 1674 and 1714 New Englanders built more than 1,200 ships, totaling at least 75,000 tons. The work employed thousands of skilled artisans, who earned good wages. Shipyards also stimulated sawmills, sail lofts, iron foundries, rope-walks, barrel shops, and taverns. And farmers benefited by feeding the artisans, victualing ships, and providing the lumber and timber to build them.

Endowed with good ships and skilled mariners, New England merchants insinuated their vessels throughout the expanding shipping lanes of the English empire, earning freight charges for goods neither produced nor consumed in New England. Ironically, for want of a plantation staple, like tobacco and sugar, New England avoided the trap of a plantation economy: the highly uneven distribution of skill and income as a labor-intensive crop polarized the population into large numbers of impoverished workers exploited by an elite. But the empire's rulers disliked colonies that could not perform the preferred colonial function of producing high-value, warm-climate agricultural staples for the homeland. Too much like the mother country in climate, resources, and people, New England competed with England's fisheries, carrying trade, and shipbuilding.

In New England, the Puritans sought to purify their churches, supervise one another, and live under laws derived from the Bible. They wanted to set an example that would inspire their countrymen in England to reform and save that kingdom from the impending divine punishment for collective sin. John Winthrop exhorted his fellow colonists to make Massachusetts "A City upon a Hill," an inspirational set of reformed churches conspicuous to the mother country. Seeking an ideal and uniform society, the Puritans certainly did not champion religious toleration and pluralism. No Catholics, Anglicans, Baptists, or Quakers need come to New England (except to exceptional Rhode Island).

The New English also felt threatened by witches, who allegedly sold their own souls to Satan for a magical power to harm and kill. Whenever cattle and children sickened and died, the New English suspected that some in their midst practiced satanic magic. For the safety of the community, witches had to be identified, prosecuted, and neutralized. The authorities pardoned suspects who confessed and testified against others, but conviction and persistent denial consigned the witch to death by hanging. Witchcraft was plausible because life was so unpredictable and because some colonists did dabble in the occult to tell fortunes and to cure, or inflict, ills (but there is scant reason to believe that any of them actually worshiped Satan). Communities disproportionately detected witchcraft among women who seemed especially angry and abrasive. Women comprised both most of the accusers and 80 percent of the accused. While attesting that the words of women had power in Puritan communities, their disproportionate prosecution also demonstrated the considerable unease generated by that power.

Rather than rush to judgment, the authorities scrupulously followed legal procedures in gathering evidence and hearing witnesses. Because it was no easy matter to prove witchcraft, juries usually acquitted. The New English prosecuted 93 witches but executed only 16—until 1692 when a peculiar mania at Salem, Massachusetts, added another 19 executions. But Puritan New England stood out because the other English colonies held few trials and probably had no executions. The Salem outburst discredited the prosecution of witches, which ceased thereafter in New England.

In addition to making enemies of religious dissidents and witches, the New English found their greatest foes among the Indians around them. The colonists saw the Indians as their opposite:

people who had surrendered to their worst instincts to live within the wild, instead of laboring hard to conquer and transcend nature. Allegedly, the Indians had succumbed to their savage land, opting for an easy and pagan life, without the hard moral discipline of Christianity or the demanding economic discipline of English civilization.

The southern New England Indians spoke related Algonkian languages, similar to those of the Virginia Indians, but they lacked political unity—and certainly had nothing like the paramount chiefdom of Powhatan. Primarily linguistic and ethnic groups, their many tribes included the Mohegan and Pequot of Connecticut; the Narragansett of Rhode Island; the Patuxet and Wampanoag of the Plymouth Colony; and the Nipmuck, Massachusett, and Pennacook of Massachusetts Bay. The tribes subdivided into many local bands, each consisting of a few hundred people sharing a horticultural village for part of the year and a common hunting and gathering territory for the rest. Highly productive crops supplied most of their diet, yet the English dismissed the Indians as mere hunters who failed to improve the land, for the newcomers failed to recognize the farming of native women.

The northeastern Algonkians acquired few material possessions and shared what they had, for their culture cherished leisure and generosity more than the laborious accumulation of individual property for conspicuous display. Honor and influence accrued to chiefs who gave away food and deerskins rather than to those who hoarded all that they could acquire.

By contrast, the English lived and worked on fixed and substantial properties, primarily framed houses and barns set among fenced fields grazed by privately owned animals. Because they showed so little generosity to their poor and less to the Algonkians, the colonists struck the natives as mean and stingy, enslaved by their property and their longings for more. The natives were also

73

astonished that the colonists so rapidly cleared the forest. The colonists needed much more cleared land primarily because they kept domesticated cattle, pigs, and sheep—in contrast to the Indians who relied on wild fish and game for their protein. The colonists also cut into the forest to obtain lumber and timber for their buildings, fences, and ships, and they ran private property lines to subdivide the land into thousands of farms that could be bought and sold. In sum, the colonists substituted an English way of living within nature for the ways that had long sustained the natives in New England.

The first major conflict between the New English and their native neighbors erupted in 1636, when the colonists tried to impose a heavy tribute on the Pequot Indians. Rebuffed, the Connecticut, Plymouth, and Massachusetts colonies declared war and pressured the Narragansett and Mohegan peoples to join the fight. In May 1637 Narragansett and Mohegan warriors guided the Puritan forces deep into the Pequot territory to surprise a palisaded village beside the Mystic River. By burning the village and shooting those who fled, the colonists killed almost all of the 600 inhabitants, most of them women, children, and old men. The indiscriminate slaughter shocked the Narragansett and Mohegan allies, who had expected to capture and adopt the women and children.

Ravaged also by disease, the disunited Indian bands became shrinking minorities in a land dominated by the rapidly growing colonial population. In 1670 the 52,000 New England colonists outnumbered the Indians of southern New England by nearly three to one. The survivors debated how best to accommodate to the powerful and demanding colonists. By 1674 about 1,600 Indians had entered Puritan missions known as "praying towns," where ministers sought to change their beliefs, behavior, and appearance. By consolidating natives in these praying towns, the Puritans sought to free up the rest of the Indian domain for their own settlements. Many of the natives saw the praying towns as their last hope for preserving their group identity on a part of their homeland. Indeed, the largest and most successful community, Natick, derived its name from an Algonkian word meaning "my land."

Most of the Indians, however, stayed away from the praying towns and resented the aggressive expansion of the settler towns. During the summer and fall of 1675, Indian rebels assailed fifty-two of the ninety towns in southern New England, destroying twelve. Armed with muskets obtained from traders, the Indians shocked the colonists with their firepower. When the colonists counterattacked, the enemy Indians took refuge in swamps and repelled their foes with heavy losses. The New Englanders blamed the uprising on a Wampanoag chief named Metacom, but known to the colonists as "King Philip." In fact, every band fought under its own leaders and to avenge their own grievances. It was those shared woes that united most of the Indians in rebellion rather than any masterful plot by Metacom.

In early 1676 the colonial leaders recognized that they needed Indian allies, which they recruited in part from the Mohegan and the surviving Pequot and, in part, from the praying towns. Facing obliteration if they refused, the praying-town Indians had to join the fight against their rebellious kin in the swamps and forests. The Puritans required their allies to prove their loyalty and zeal by bringing in two scalps or heads taken from the enemy. Because a third of the region's natives assisted the colonists, King Philip's War became a civil war among the natives.

During the spring and summer of 1676, New England's native allies helped turn the tide of war in favor of the colonists. Running low on food and ammunition, the resistance collapsed, as one demoralized group after another surrendered. In August, a praying-town Indian shot the fleeing Metacom, and the colonists cut off his head for display on a post atop a brick watchtower in Plymouth. The colonists executed some of the captured chiefs and enslaved their families for sale in the West

Indies or the Mediterranean. Those sold included Metacom's wife and nine-year-old son.

The conflict had killed at least 1,000 English colonists and about 3,000 Indians, a quarter of their population in southern New England. Some of the defeated rebels escaped northward to take refuge among the Abenaki Indians in northern New England and New France. The refugees carried with them a bitter hatred of the New Englanders, returning in future wars to raid their frontier settlements. The colonists' Indian allies persisted in southern New England as a small and maligned minority, dwelling on a few shrinking reservations surrounded by the colonial towns.

New England was a land of relative equality, broad (albeit moderate) opportunity, and thrifty, industrious, and entrepreneurial habits. The colonists sustained an especially diverse and developed economy. The region's large, healthy families, nearly even gender ratio, and long life spans promoted social stability and the slow but steady accumulation of property. And nowhere else in the colonies did colonists enjoy readier access to public worship and education. But those accomplishments had a dark side: the persecution of dissenters and suspected witches, and their dispossession of the Indians.

Chapter 6
West Indies and Carolina

Although few New Englanders owned slaves, their farms and ships serviced the slave-based economy of the West Indies: a set of fertile subtropical islands that framed the Caribbean Sea in an arc sweeping northward from South America and then westward beneath Florida. During the 1620s and early 1630s, the West Indies evolved from temporary bases for pirates into permanent colonies for planters. Devoting almost all of their land to raising tobacco or sugar cane, the West Indian planters had to import food and lumber from New England. In effect, seventeenth-century New England and the English West Indies developed in tandem as mutually sustaining parts of a common economic system. Each was incomplete without the other.

By producing sugar, the West Indies became the most valuable set of English colonies. Sugar could bear the costs of long-distance transportation (and the purchase of slaves by the thousand) because of the great and growing European demand to sweeten food and drink. Requiring a year-round growing season, fertile soil, and abundant water, sugarcane thrived in subtropical colonies rather than in Europe. In 1686, the West Indian exports to England were three times as valuable as all of the commodities shipped there from the mainland colonies of North America. Chesapeake tobacco was valuable to the empire—indeed, more precious than all other mainland produce combined—but West Indian sugar was king in the empire.

Despite their small size, the islands received most of the English emigrants to the Americas during the early seventeenth century. In 1650 more white colonists lived in the West Indies (44,000) than in the Chesapeake (12,000) and New England colonies (23,000) combined (35,000). Two-thirds of the English West Indians then lived on the single island of Barbados although it was only twenty-one miles long and fourteen miles wide. As in the Chesapeake, most of the West Indian immigrants were poor, single young men who arrived as indentured servants. Those who survived their five-year-long indentures obtained freedom and about five acres of land and the provisions, clothing, and tools to become small-scale farmers. Prior to 1640, they cultivated tobacco and raised livestock (hides) for export to Europe, while growing, for their own subsistence, corn, cassava, yams, plantains, and sweet potatoes.

During the 1640s, Barbadians shifted toward cultivating sugarcane and manufacturing sugar. By 1660 Barbados made most of the sugar consumed in England and generated more trade and capital than all other English colonies combined. To perform the long, hard work of raising sugarcane and making sugar, the planters imported thousands of slaves from Africa. By 1645 the £20 cost for a slave compared favorably to the £12 required to purchase just five years of indentured labor. The buyer of slaves also never had to pay the "freedom dues" owed to the servant at the expiration of his indenture. And, in contrast to servants, the children of a slave woman became the property of her master, providing additional returns on the original investment.

By 1660 Barbados became the first English colony with a black and enslaved majority: 27,000 compared to 26,000 whites. More slaves dwelled on Barbados than in all other English colonies combined. Indeed, the Chesapeake colonies had only 900 slaves in 1660 (about 4 percent of the total population). As slaves proliferated on Barbados, indentured servitude dwindled. By 1680 the island had seventeen slaves for every indentured servant.

The growing slave population depended on increased human imports, for the Barbadian slaves died far faster than they could reproduce. The slaves succumbed to a deadly combination of tropical diseases, a brutal work regimen, and the inadequate diet, housing, and clothing provided by their masters. Rather than improve those conditions, the Barbadian planters found it more profitable to import slaves even faster than they could be worked to death. Although the planters brought 130,000 Africans into Barbados between 1640 and 1700, only 50,000 remained alive there at the dawn of the new century.

Sugar was a rich man's crop, for small operations could not compete in the markets to acquire land, labor, and equipment. Acquiring and capitalizing a 100-acre plantation cost at least £2,000—too expensive for all but the rich in a century where few hired laborers made more than £10 in a year. Consequently, competition drove the smaller planters out of business, concentrating large plantations in fewer and richer hands. By 1680 more than half of the arable land on Barbados belonged to the richest 7 percent of the free colonists. This small elite commanded, on average, 115 slaves, 250 acres, and a net worth of £4,000. Once a land of apparent promise for common tobacco planters, Barbados had become the domain of sugar grandees and their African slaves.

While the black population grew, the white numbers declined, as most of the common freed men either died of disease or moved away in search of their own land. Squeezed out of Barbados, thousands emigrated to the less developed islands of Nevis, St. Kitts, Montserrat, and Antigua or farther west to Jamaica, which became their principal destination. Located 1,000 miles east of the Lesser Antilles, Jamaica was an especially large island of 4,400 square miles: ten times bigger than the rest of the English

West Indies combined. Lacking the capital and slaves for sugar, the small planters raised cattle and pigs, and cultivated small fields of indigo, cotton, and cacao.

During the 1690s, however, Jamaica repeated the transformation that had driven the small planters from Barbados. About 10,000 in 1690, the number of Jamaican whites declined to 7,000 by 1713. Meanwhile, slave imports surged, swelling the black population to 55,000, eight times larger than the white numbers. In 1713 Jamaica produced more sugar than Barbados, becoming the wealthiest and most important colony in the English empire.

Paradoxically, Jamaica also sustained the largest population of *Maroons*—runaway slaves living in autonomous communities—in the English West Indies. In contrast to crowded and deforested Barbados, where the runaways found scant place to hide, Jamaica offered refuges in the densely vegetated Blue Mountains of the northeast and the rugged "Cockpit Country" of the west-center. The Jamaican *Maroons* raided plantations and ambushed pursuers until the colonial authorities agreed to leave them alone, provided that they stopped their raids and returned future runaways. In effect, the *Maroons* sustained free communities in the recesses of a colony dedicated to plantation slavery, but they considered themselves as distinct communities with special rights—rather than as the vanguard of a general racial uprising. Indeed, rival *Maroon* bands sometimes attacked and killed one another, and as slave catchers, they helped to keep the slave majority at work on their plantations. But the *Maroon* example also inspired new rebellions on isolated plantations, where the slaves sought to escape into the mountains to found their own free communities. If they could outrun and outfight pursuit for a few years, they too could win *Maroon* status—but *Maroons* accounted for only 1 percent of Jamaica's black population.

By 1700 the West Indian colonies featured a small but rich planter elite, a marginal population of poor whites, a great majority of black slaves, and a few defiant *Maroons*. The population grew only by a massive importation of new slaves. Between 1640 and 1700, the English West Indies acquired about 260,000 slaves, but only 100,000 of them were still alive in 1700. Although an economic success, the West Indies was a demographic failure that manifested a society in consuming pursuit of profit and with a callous disregard for life.

Some white emigrants sought new lands on the southern mainland of North America. In 1670 three ships from Barbados bore 200 colonists north to the mouth of the Ashley River, where they founded Charles Town (later changed to "Charleston"), which became the seaport and capital of the new colony of Carolina and which included present-day North and South Carolina and Georgia. The founders named the town and colony to honor King Charles II. The eight official owners, known as the Lords Proprietor, were aristocrats who remained in England, entrusting the colonization to Barbadians. The abundant lands of Carolina appealed to the crowded discontent and frustrated ambitions of West Indian white men.

The new colony boldly defied Spanish claims to that coast— signifying the new English confidence in their emerging imperial power as the Spanish grew weaker. Early in the seventeenth century, the English had felt obliged to hide their Jamestown colony up a distant river, but in 1670 the English defiantly planted Charles Town near the coast on the very margins of Florida.

To secure Carolina from Spanish attack, the Lords Proprietor needed to attract many colonists. To entice newcomers, the Lords promised religious toleration; political representation in an assembly with control over public taxation and expenditures; and generous grants of land, generally 150 acres for each member of a free white family. The incentives worked. From 200 colonists in 1670, South Carolina grew to about 6,600 in 1700 (3,800 white and 2,800 black). The new colony became more than a match for the 1,500 Spanish in Florida.

During the late seventeenth century, Carolina offered the frontier combination of opportunity and danger that had been lost in Barbados as it became more crowded and developed. In Carolina, the male servant who survived his term received the customary "freedom dues"—a set of clothes, a barrel of corn, an axe, and a hoe—from his master and a land grant from the Lords Proprietor.

In addition to common settlers, the colony attracted great planters with the capital and the slaves to speed development. To encourage them, the Lords Proprietor allowed a master to claim a full 150-acre headright for each slave imported. From the West Indies, the wealthiest of the new colonists settled on Goose Creek near Charles Town. Known as the "Goose Creek Men," they dominated the assembly and council of Carolina. They conducted politics in the Barbadian style, characterized by the unrestrained pursuit of self-interest and the ruthless exploitation of others. Arrogant and Anglican, the Goose Creek Men stifled the policy of religious toleration in 1702 by reserving political offices for Anglicans and by requiring all planters to pay taxes to that church. During the 1720s, the Goose Creek Men defied the Lords Proprietor to transform Carolina into a royal colony with a governor appointed by the Crown.

As a plantation colony in a frontier setting, the Carolinians needed to dominate both enslaved Africans and defiant Indians, lest they combine to merge slave rebellion with frontier war. The colonists sought to pit the Africans against the Indians, the better to exploit both. In their treaties with native peoples, the colonists insisted upon the return of all fugitives as the price of peace and trade. As a further incentive, Carolina paid bounties to Indians who captured and returned runaways, at the rate of one gun and three blankets for each.

Carolina's early leaders concluded that the key to managing the local Indians was to offer them guns and ammunition in trade for their deerskins and captives. Far from undermining colonial security, the gun trade rendered the natives dependent upon weapons that they could neither make nor repair. If deprived of ammunition, the natives would suffer in their hunting and fall prey to slave-raiding by better-armed Indians more favored by a colonial supplier. And thanks to the superiority of British manufactures and shipping, the Carolina trader enjoyed the advantages of both quality and quantity in his competition with the French and the Spanish.

By pushing the gun and slave trade and building a network of native allies, the Carolinians secured their own frontier and wreaked havoc on the more distant Indians affiliated with the Spanish and French. The raids spread death and destruction hundreds of miles beyond Carolina, west to the Mississippi and south into Florida. The traders preferred women and children as captives, deeming them more adaptable to a new life as slaves. Indian men tended to die resisting attacks, or they were executed upon surrender. The Carolinians employed some captives on their own plantations, which in 1708 held 1,400 native as well as 2,900 African slaves. But native captives might escape into the nearby forest, so the Carolinians exported most of them to the West Indies in exchange for Africans.

The Carolina traders especially encouraged their Indian allies to attack the Spanish missions in Florida, where the poorly armed and conveniently clustered Guale, Timucua, and Apalachee proved easy pickings. During the 1680s, Savannah, Creek, and Yamasee raiders destroyed the Guale missions along the coast of Georgia. Between 1704 and 1706 the raiders destroyed another thirty-two native villages and their missions, inflicting horrific casualties and enslaving thousands. Most of the captured Spanish priests were tortured to death, and their churches went up in flames. Florida's Indian population collapsed from about 16,000 in 1685 to 3,700

West Indies and Carolina

83

in 1715, and the missions shrank to a few in the immediate vicinity and partial security of San Agustín. The Carolina gun and slave trade had triumphed over the Spanish mission system as an instrument of colonial power. Without the missions, Spanish Florida became a hollow shell, while English Carolina became the leading regional power.

After the destruction of the Florida missions, potential captives became scarcer and the Indian allies fell into arrears on their debts owed to the Carolina traders. Natives who rebelled or who tried to flee the region became the targets of slave raids encouraged by the traders and inflicted by their allies. In 1707 the Savannah Indians were crushed, with a minority escaping north to refuge in Pennsylvania. In 1711 the Tuscarora, Iroquoian-speakers who lived in North Carolina, lashed out, destroying frontier farms. But the colonists and their allies stormed and burned the Tuscarora villages, killing and enslaving hundreds. Most of the survivors fled northward to New York, taking refuge among the Haudenosaunee, becoming their Sixth Nation. Almost immediately after helping to destroy the Tuscarora, the Yamasee rebelled, killing traders, slaughtering cattle, and burning frontier plantations. But, as in King Philip's War in New England, the Carolina Indian rebels lost momentum as they ran low on guns and gunpowder. And trade goods enticed other Indians—Catawba, Chickasaw, and Cherokee—to help crush the Yamasee.

In 1700 Indian numbers had nearly equaled the colonists and their slaves in Carolina: 15,000 natives, compared to 16,000 colonists and Africans. By 1730, however, the 37,000 white colonists and 27,000 blacks in South and North Carolina had surged far beyond the local Indian population, which had collapsed to just 4,000. Very little of the native decline derived from direct conflict between colonists and Indians, but the population collapse had everything to do with the indirect consequences of the colonial intrusion. The Carolina Indians dwindled from a catastrophic combination of disease epidemics, rum consumption, and slave-raid violence.

Colonial traders introduced all three, the disease unintentionally, but the alcohol and raiding by design.

In addition to trading for deerskins and Indian slaves, the Carolinians raised livestock and harvested lumber, pitch, and tar from the thick forests. Carolinians pioneered many practices later perfected on a grand scale in the American West, including cattle branding, annual round-ups, cow pens, and cattle drives from the interior to the market in Charles Town.

Despite their modest success as ranchers and loggers, aspiring Carolinians continued to experiment with more valuable crops. During the 1690s, they developed rice as their great staple for the export market. A subtropical grain, rice thrived in the wet lowlands of Carolina. With slave labor, the planters re-engineered the extensive tidewater swamps, diking out the tide to reserve freshwater for the rice. The annual rice exports surged from 400,000 pounds in 1700 to about 43 million in 1740, when rice comprised over 60 percent of the total exports from Carolina as measured by value. Carolina became the empire's great rice colony—just as the Chesapeake specialized in tobacco and the West Indies in sugar. Enjoying a protected market within the empire for rice, Carolina planters became the wealthiest colonial elite on the Atlantic seaboard. Of course, that wealth depended upon the lands taken from Indians and the hard labor extorted from Africans.

As the planters cultivated more rice, they imported more slaves, the one paying for—and making necessary—the other. While North Carolina retained a white majority, in South Carolina the slaves outnumbered the free, white colonists by two to one. The African majority became concentrated in the rice-growing district: the hot, humid, marshy, lowlands of the coastal plain. As in the West Indies, the black majority preserved many African traditions and languages and built their quarters in African style. As in Barbados, so in Carolina, the brutal working conditions and the disease-ridden lowland environment produced slave mortality rates in excess of their birth rate. Only the ongoing African imports sustained the steady growth of the slave population in Carolina.

As in the West Indies, the Carolina planters suffered from a haunting fear that their African majority would rise up in deadly, burning rebellion. Convulsed by rumors of murderous plots, the terrified authorities employed torture to obtain confessions, which led to executions, sometimes by hanging but usually by burning at the stake. These spectacles hardly abated the fear that nagged at every master.

On Sunday, September 9, 1739, the dread became real in a slave rebellion on the Stono River, twenty miles from Charles Town. Twenty slaves plundered a store of guns and gunpowder. Marching south, they hoped to reach Spanish Florida, which welcomed runaway slaves from Carolina by bestowing freedom and land. En route, the rebels burned seven plantations and attracted another eighty supporters by displaying a makeshift flag, beating two drums, and chanting "Liberty!" But the whites had the advantages of horses, more guns, better training in arms, and a militia command structure. On the second day of the uprising, about a hundred armed and mounted white militiamen surprised and routed the rebels, killing most, usually after they had surrendered. To terrify the other slaves, the victors cut off the rebels' heads and placed them on posts, one every mile, between the battlefield and Charles Town. But no matter how repressively they ruled, or how cowed the Africans behaved, the masters still dreaded that their slaves would kill to be free.

To increase South Carolina's security against Spanish Florida, the British had recently established a new colony along the Savannah River. Named "Georgia," in honor of King George II, the new colony was entrusted to a set of London philanthropists and social reformers led by General James Oglethorpe. In 1733 Oglethorpe led the first Georgia colonists across the Atlantic to found the town of Savannah, on a bluff near the mouth of that river.

The "Georgia Trustees" hoped to alleviate English urban poverty by shipping imprisoned debtors to their new colony, where hard work on their own farms would cure indolence. By this moral alchemy, people who drained English charity would become productive subjects working both to improve themselves and to defend the empire on a valuable but vulnerable frontier. In effect, the trustees revived the scheme of the sixteenth-century West Country promoters, who had proposed Virginia as a colonial workhouse to redeem England's sturdy beggars. From 1733 to 1742 the trustees freely transported, and provided small farms to, about 1,800 charity colonists. Other immigrants paid their own way, lured by the prospect of free land.

The trustees wanted a colony of many compact farms worked by free families instead of one with larger but fewer plantations dependent upon enslaved Africans. In other words, the trustees sought to prevent Georgia from becoming like Carolina. By maximizing the number of white militiamen, the trustees tried to enhance security against attack by Indians or the Spanish. Moreover, black slavery made manual labor seem degrading to white men, who aspired, instead, to acquire their own slaves to do the dirty work. Consequently, slavery threatened to corrode the labor discipline that the trustees meant to teach to the Georgia colonists.

Georgia was the first and only colony to reject the slave system so fundamental and profitable to the rest of the British Empire. Driven by concerns for military security and white moral uplift, the antislavery policy expressed neither a principled empathy for enslaved Africans nor an ambition to emancipate slaves elsewhere. Indeed, by securing the southern frontier, Georgia promised to strengthen slavery in Carolina by closing an escape hatch to Florida that invited both slave flight and rebellion.

These restrictions rankled the more ambitious colonists, who resented the trustees as unrealistic, unresponsive, and dictatorial. Frustrated and impatient, the settlers contrasted their hardships and poverty with the relative ease and prosperity of the whites in Carolina. Seeking a quick fix, the discontented settlers became fixated on the antislavery ban as the chief obstacle to their ambitions. The Georgia malcontents rallied behind the slogan, "Liberty and Property without restrictions"—which insisted that white men could be free only if allowed to hold blacks as property. This seems hypocritical to modern readers committed to universal principles of human rights, but the reasoning made sense in an eighteenth-century empire where liberty was a privileged status that depended upon the power to subordinate someone else.

8. Gentlemen of the Manigault family—one of the most prominent in eighteenth-century Charleston—gather to drink and toast. The Manigaults made their fortune as rice planters and merchants.

In 1751 the trustees gave up, surrendering Georgia to the Crown, which permitted slavery. The rapid development of rice and indigo plantations spurred a surge in immigration, principally by Carolinians bringing in slaves. From about 3,000 whites and 600 blacks in 1752, Georgia's population surged to 18,000 whites and 15,000 blacks in 1775. As in the West Indies and in Carolina, a planter elite became immensely rich, leisured, and politically powerful by exploiting enslaved Africans and Indian land.

Because the society of Georgia and Carolina so closely resembled Barbados, imperial officials commonly referred to the region as "Carolina in the West Indies." Plantation society had driven from Barbados the emigrants who became the first Carolinians. But they went to Carolina with no radical vision of an egalitarian alternative to the staple and slave system of the West Indies. On the contrary, the emigrants sought their own place to achieve the mastery and wealth of great planters.

Chapter 7
British America

Compared to other empires, the English monarch exercised little power over his colonists, primarily because during the early seventeenth century, the then underfunded Crown had entrusted colonization to private interests licensed by royal charters. Those charters awarded the proprietors not only title to colonial territories as landlords but also the rights to govern the colonists—subject to royal oversight, which was sporadic at best. In a few colonies, principally Virginia, the Crown had taken control away from the proprietors.

In each colony, either the Crown (in the royal colonies) or proprietors (in the proprietary colonies) appointed a governor and council, but propertied colonists insisted upon electing an assembly with power over the colonial finances. Propertied Englishmen cherished legislative control over taxation as their most fundamental liberty. By virtue of their especially indulgent charters, the New England colonies were virtually independent of Crown authority and of any external proprietors. Consequently, New England developed republican regimes where the landowners elected their governors and councils as well as their assemblies and where much decision-making was dispersed to the many small towns.

During the later seventeenth century, the Crown sought tighter control over the colonies, the better to regulate and tax their commerce—and the better to defend them. King Charles II and his brother, James, the Duke of York, perceived the colonies as too small, weak, and too fractious in their reliance on elected assemblies. Imperial bureaucrats sought to convert most of the proprietary colonies into royal colonies, with crown-appointed governors and councils, and then to consolidate them into an overarching government like the Spanish viceroyalty of New Spain.

England's imperial officials recognized the connection, pioneered by the Dutch, between overseas colonies, commercial expansion, and national power. By emulating the Dutch, the English set out to eclipse and to replace them as the dominant power in the trade of the world. As one small step in that direction, in 1664 the Crown sent a naval squadron with soldiers across the Atlantic to attack the Dutch colony of New Netherland located along the Hudson River.

New Netherland was a minor colony of an especially wealthy, ambitious, and far-flung empire that had burgeoned early in the century. The Netherlands became an economic and military giant, out of all proportion to its confined homeland and small population of 1.5 million (compared to 5 million English and 20 million French). Thanks to an efficient merchant marine and fishing fleet, the Dutch dominated the carrying trade of northern and western Europe, the North Seas fisheries, and Arctic whaling. In 1670 the Dutch employed 120,000 sailors on vessels totaling 568,000 tons—more than the combined shipping of Spain, France, and England.

The Dutch economy also benefited from a liberal government that adopted policies of intellectual freedom and religious toleration unique in seventeenth-century Europe. While the other leading European states were developing powerful and centralized monarchies, the Dutch opted for a decentralized republic dominated by wealthy merchants and rural aristocrats. The Dutch attracted religious minorities ousted by the repression practiced in the other European realms. By enticing French Protestants and

Iberian and German Jews, the Dutch reaped their talents and investments. The combination of republican government, religious toleration, naval power, colonial trade, and manufacturing boom endowed the Dutch with the greatest national wealth and the highest standard of living in Europe.

The Protestant Dutch built their empire by rebelling against their sixteenth-century rulers, the Catholic Spanish. To weaken their enemy and to reap profits, Dutch warships preyed on Spanish and Portuguese shipping and colonies in the East and West Indies. By 1650 the Dutch had seized primacy in the importation of tea and spices from Asia, the export of sugar from American plantations, and in the slave trade from West Africa.

During the early seventeenth century, the Dutch also founded New Netherland, which consisted of a riverside string of farms between a small, upriver fur-trading post, Fort Orange (now Albany), and a fortified seaport, New Amsterdam, on Manhattan Island near the mouth of the river. The seaport protected the colony from naval attack, while the farms in the lower valley fed the fur traders upriver. In 1655 the Dutch conquered New Sweden, an even smaller Swedish colony in the nearby Delaware valley to the west. The Dutch West India Company appointed the governor and an advisory council of leading colonists but permitted no elected assembly. In addition to the Dutch, the colony attracted immigrants from Belgium (Flemings and Walloons), France (Huguenots), Scandinavia, Germany, and New England. The non-Dutch comprised at least three-fifths of the colonists.

But New Netherland attracted relatively few colonists: only 5,000 by 1660, better than the 3,000 in New France but far behind the 25,000 in the Chesapeake and the 33,000 in New England. In transatlantic migration, push was stronger than pull, and that push was far stronger in England than in the Netherlands. Blessed with religious toleration, a booming economy, and a higher standard of living, the Dutch had fewer reasons to leave home than did the English, who were suffering through religious conflicts, a civil war, and a stagnant economy. Thinly populated, New Netherland proved vulnerable when the Dutch and English empires came to blows.

To build up English trade at the Dutch expense, Parliament adopted a series of Navigation Acts during the 1650s and 1660s. Mandating that only English ships could trade with any English colony, the acts defined as English any ship built within the empire, owned and captained by an English subject, and sailed by a crew at least three-quarters English. Because the colonists were English subjects, their ships and sailors fell within the definition. Any trade open to the merchants and mariners of the mother country was equally open to their colonists. The acts also stipulated that the most valuable colonial commodities— primarily tobacco and sugar—could be shipped only to the mother country and in the ships of English subjects. And the acts stipulated that all European goods carried to the colonies had to pass through an English port, where they paid customs duties.

The Navigation Acts sought to (1) maximize customs revenue collected in England; (2) increase the flow of commerce enriching English merchants; (3) stimulate English shipbuilding; and (4) augment the number of English sailors, swelling the reserve for the navy. Enforced by that expanding navy, the Navigation Acts boosted the English share of overseas commerce, and merchant shipping more than doubled from 150,000 tons in 1640 to 340,000 in 1686.

By threatening the Dutch economy, the Navigation Acts provoked three Anglo-Dutch wars between 1652 and 1674. In 1664 an English fleet and troops captured New Netherland. Nine years later, during the third war, the Dutch briefly recaptured their colony, but they surrendered it for good in the peace treaty of 1674. The Dutch colony of New Netherland became the English colony of New York, New Amsterdam became New York City, and Fort Orange became Albany.

King Charles II entrusted New York to his brother, James, the Duke of York, as the proprietor. The duke then set aside the lands between the Hudson and the Delaware Rivers to create the colonies of East and West Jersey, later merged to form "New Jersey." By 1700 policies of religious toleration and elected assemblies had attracted 14,000 colonists: a mix of English Quakers, New English Puritans, and Scots Presbyterians.

To pay off a large debt, in 1680 the king granted 45,000 square miles on the west side of the Delaware River to William Penn, who named his proprietary colony "Pennsylvania." Although born to great wealth, Penn had espoused Quakerism, an especially mystical, radical, and persecuted form of Protestantism. Quakers carried the Puritan critiques of church hierarchy and ritual to their ultimate conclusion: a rejection of all sacraments, liturgies, and paid intermediaries—ministers as well as bishops—between a soul and God. Renouncing formal prayers, sermons, and ceremony of any sort, Quakers met together as spiritual equals and sat silently until the divine spirit inspired someone to speak. They relied on mystical experience in search of an "Inner Light" to understand the Bible. To emphasize their equality in the eyes of God, the Quakers wore plain clothes, refused to take oaths of allegiance or for testimony, rejected the payment of church tithes, used plain, familiar language with all people, even to address aristocrats or the king, and declined to doff their hats before their rulers as a conventional sign of respect. Considering women spiritually equal to men, Quakers established parallel men's and women's leadership for their meetings. As pacifists, the Quakers refused to bear arms.

In 1682 Penn began to settle Pennsylvania by founding Philadelphia, the "City of Brotherly Love," at the juncture of the Schuylkill River with the Delaware River. Committed to religious

9. William Penn founded the Quaker colony of Pennsylvania in 1682. Unlike most founders of American colonies, Penn extended equal rights to European settlers of all religious persuasions.

toleration, Penn welcomed non-Quakers as well as Quakers to Pennsylvania, promising equal rights and opportunities to all. His colony would have no privileged church, no tax-supported religious establishment. In addition to a majority of English or Welsh Quakers, the colony attracted English Anglicans and German pietists.

Pennsylvania quickly prospered as a farm colony settled by families of middling means. In contrast to rocky New England, southeastern Pennsylvania possessed a fertile soil and an easily tilled landscape of low, rolling hills, where the colonists thrived by raising wheat and livestock for export. Because Penn treated Indians with restraint and respect, Pennsylvania also enjoyed prolonged peace with the local Indians, avoiding the sort of native rebellions that had temporarily devastated Virginia, New England, and New Mexico. Indeed, the local Lenni Lenape (or "Delawares") welcomed Penn as a colonial patron who could provide trade goods.

Despite the peace, prosperity, and religious toleration, Pennsylvania suffered from political conflict. Resisting Penn's authoritarian paternalism, most of the colonists wanted a powerful assembly to restrict the power of their proprietor. Dissidents insisted that Penn had fleeced and restricted most of the colonists to further enrich himself and his cronies. Feeling betrayed by the criticism, Penn denounced his opponents as selfish ingrates indifferent to his extraordinary exertions in colonizing Pennsylvania.

During the last third of the seventeenth century, the English developed a new cluster of colonies—New York, New Jersey, Pennsylvania, and its southern satellite, Delaware—in the mid-Atlantic region. Because these colonies lay between New England to the north and the Chesapeake to the south, the new region became known as "the Middle Colonies." The ethnic and denominational diversity of the region anticipated the American future, but the fractious contentions of those groups frustrated English visions of an empire responsive to command, especially during war.

In early 1685 King Charles II died and left his throne to his younger brother, who reigned as James II. A vigorous, zealous, and tactless king, James openly practiced his unpopular Catholicism and vowed to rule as an absolute monarch without consulting Parliament. By seeking a larger revenue from the colonies, the new king hoped to dispense with Parliament, which was constitutionally necessary to levy new taxes within England. James especially wanted to reduce New England to obedience, for those colonies often evaded the Navigation Acts so critical to the power and revenue of the Crown.

Revoking their government charters, James consolidated the eight northern colonies—all five in New England plus New York and East and West Jersey—into a supercolony known as the Dominion of New England. Modeled on a Spanish viceroyalty, the Dominion extended from the Delaware River to Canada. The Dominion dispensed with assemblies, entrusting administration to a governor-general assisted by a lieutenant governor and an appointed council. For governor-general, the king appointed Sir Edmund Andros, a military officer who established his capitol in Boston. Andros replaced local judges and militia officers with Anglican newcomers. He also appointed the county sheriffs, who named the jurors—which did not bode well for the rights of defendants. More expensive than the old charter governments, the Dominion demanded higher taxes from colonists newly deprived of their assemblies.

But James suffered a sudden fall from power in 1688, when William, the Dutch and Protestant Prince of Orange, invaded England with a Dutch army and the encouragement of Anglican bishops and aristocrats. The English troops refused to fight, so James II fled to France, while Parliament transferred the throne to William and his wife Mary (the daughter of James). Although they ruled as joint sovereigns, Mary left governance to her husband. The new monarchs promised to cooperate with Parliament and to favor Protestants, who celebrated the coup as "the Glorious Revolution."

The Crown and Parliament formed a new partnership to fund the expanded army and navy needed to defend their joint regime against James and his French patrons. Formerly a bulwark against unpopular taxes and Crown power, Parliament became the great collection agency for the Protestant regime and a transatlantic empire. In return for heavy new taxes and a standing army, Parliament demanded and got greater control over expenditures. That new fiscal control enabled Parliament to guide foreign and military policy, previously jealously guarded as royal prerogatives. In effect, national sovereignty became vested in Parliament as well as in the Crown in a formula called the "King-in-Parliament."

Meanwhile, in 1689 in the colonies, news of the Glorious Revolution had inspired colonial dissidents to stage their own coups. In Boston, armed rebels arrested Andros and his officials in April of that year. A month later, New York's militia seized the fort and sent Andros's lieutenant, Francis Nicholson, back to England. In August, in Maryland, the Protestant majority led by John Coode seized power from the Catholic governor appointed by their proprietor, Lord Baltimore. In New York and New England, the rebels dissolved the Dominion and restored separate governments under their old charters. Pledging loyalty to the empire, they looked to the new monarchs to approve their actions.

A pragmatic ruler, William III recognized that he had to compromise with the colonial leaders to encourage their cooperation with his imperial plans to wage war on France. To the delight of the Maryland rebels, the new king appointed a royal governor to take charge of Maryland away from Lord Baltimore. In Massachusetts, the king refused to restore the old charter and, instead, imposed a new, compromise charter that mandated both a royal governor and an elected assembly. He also strengthened that colony by dissolving the small Plymouth colony for incorporation into Massachusetts. Rather than bother with the smaller New England colonies, the Crown simply let Rhode Island and Connecticut revive their old charters and autonomy.

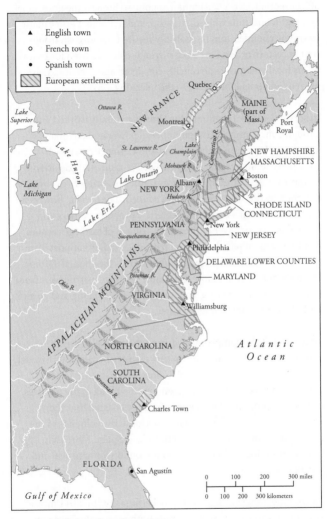

10. The Atlantic seaboard, ca. 1700.

Compromise proved most elusive in New York, where a militia officer named Jacob Leisler had appointed himself the governor. Self-righteous, inflexible, distrustful, and irritable, Leisler made too many enemies, and he foolishly resisted the English troops sent to restore order. Forced to surrender, he was tried for treason by his local enemies, who quickly convicted and executed Leisler to prevent an appeal for mercy to the new king.

In sorting out the rebellions, the Crown generally worked out a rough compromise between imperial power and colonial autonomy. Except in Rhode Island and Connecticut, which were petty republics, the colonies had to submit all legislation to approval first by their governors (either proprietary or royal) and then by the king and his privy council. The Crown, however, accepted colonial assemblies elected by property holders and blessed with the power of the purse. Instead of force, governors had to rely upon persuasion and patronage to buy support from the leading colonists in the assembly and on the council. Often the governors had to ignore their more coercive instructions from London upon discovering that it was best to get along and go along with the leaders in their assemblies.

As a result of the compromise, during the early eighteenth century, the colonies and the mother country became more closely intertwined in a shared empire. Colonial leaders insisted that they were transplanted English endowed with all of the liberties enjoyed by propertied men at home. They boasted that their English liberties rendered them superior to the colonists of the more authoritarian empires of France and Spain. More than ever before, ambitious colonists looked to London for approval and patronage.

In 1707 the hitherto English empire became the "British Empire" with the absorption of Scotland into a common realm based in London. In return for losing their own Parliament, the Scots won access to the thriving colonies founded by the English.

Scots gentlemen became numerous and conspicuous as colonial officials and governors. Scots merchants also captured a growing share in the colonial commerce, especially the tobacco trade from the Chesapeake. And between 1707 and 1775, about 145,000 Scots crossed the Atlantic to replace the English as the primary immigrants to the colonies. During the same period, English emigration declined sharply to only 80,000, compared to 350,000 during the preceding century. Despite the lower cost of transatlantic travel, fewer English emigrated after 1700, because the economy at home had begun to grow, modestly boosting the real wages for laboring families, enabling more to remain in the mother country.

Poorer than the English, the Scots had greater incentives to emigrate, and they enjoyed new access thanks to the British Union. Nearly half of the Scots emigrants came from Ulster, in Northern Ireland, where their parents and grandparents had colonized during the preceding generation. During the 1710s and 1720s they suffered from a depressed market for their linen, the hunger of several poor harvests, and the increased rents charged by grasping landlords.

In addition to Scots, British America attracted a new surge of 100,000 Germans, who also outnumbered the English as eighteenth-century colonial immigrants. Most were Protestants, but they divided into multiple denominations: Lutherans, Reformed, Moravians, Baptists, and Pietists of many stripes. Primarily from the Rhine valley, they crossed the Atlantic via the Dutch port of Rotterdam and landed at Philadelphia, the great magnet for colonial immigration. The migrants sought relief from the chronic wars that ravaged Germany; they also fled from princes who demanded military conscripts and religious conformity from their subjects, inflicting fines and imprisonment on dissidents. News of the abundant, fertile land in Pennsylvania also drew these discontented Germans across the Atlantic. Lacking princes and aristocrats or an established church, Pennsylvania demanded almost no taxes—and none to support someone else's religion. In addition, Pennsylvania did not conscript its inhabitants for war.

But most of the immigrants to eighteenth-century British America did not come by their own free will in search of liberty, nor were they Europeans. Instead, most were enslaved Africans forced across the Atlantic to work on plantations raising American crops for the European market. During the eighteenth century, the British colonies imported 1,500,000 slaves— more than three times the number of free immigrants. British America was a land of black slavery as well as a land of white opportunity.

A brutal business, the slave trade killed about 10 percent of the slaves in transit. The survivors then suffered the shock of enslavement in a strange and distant new land. Separated from friends and kin, they were ordered about in a new language and brutally punished if they balked or resisted. Arriving with many distinct languages and identities, they had to form a new culture as African Americans. Meanwhile, they suffered from the minimal food, shelter, and ragged clothing provided by their profit-seeking masters driven to lower their costs. As a rule, the slaves had to work at least twelve hours a day, six days a week under the close supervision and sharp whip of a white overseer. Masters and overseers compelled enough labor and obedience to profit from the slave system, but they did so with greater difficulty and chronic fear of a slave revolt.

About three-quarters of the new slaves went to the West Indies, where the sugar plantations were especially profitable but deadly, so it paid masters to work slaves to death and then to replace them. In the mainland colonies, however, the masters made a greater effort to provide minimal housing and food to keep their slaves alive and reproducing. The largest number lived in the Chesapeake, where they comprised about 40 percent of the total population in 1775. Although legal in every colony, African slaves were only 2 percent of the population in New England and 8 percent in the Middle Colonies.

As British America became more ethnically and racially diverse, the free colonists became more closely tied to the economy and culture of the mother country. Although colonists often protested some feature of the Navigation Acts, none wanted an abolition of the whole system. Indeed, the colonists benefited from the mother country as a protected market for the produce of their farms and plantations, while the British manufacturers increasingly relied on colonial consumers.

Far from dividing the colonists from the mother country, the Atlantic Ocean drew them closer together during the early to mid-eighteenth century. Thanks to a tripling in the number of transatlantic voyages, colonists became significantly better informed about events in, and ideas from, Britain and especially London. The swelling volume of shipping also boosted the colonial economy, which grew faster than did that of the mother country. From just 4 percent of England's gross domestic product in 1700, the colonial economy blossomed to 40 percent by 1770, assuming a much greater importance to the empire. Thanks to substantial farms and booming trade, most of the free colonists enjoyed a higher standard of living than did the common people in Europe. The rising incomes enabled colonists to purchase more British manufactured goods—which reinforced the economic ties between the mother country and the colonies.

During the eighteenth century, the expanding transatlantic commerce produced a "consumer revolution," which meant cheaper and more diverse goods in greater abundance. At the same time, demand swelled as colonial consumers sought a wider array of new things, especially Asian tea and spices, and British manufactured goods. Women played a leading role in the consumer revolution, for the imported goods reduced their long and hard labor to spin thread and to weave cloth. By acquiring fashionable clothing, middle-class women also obtained a new means for self-expression and self-assertion. In vain, old-fashioned newspaper writers denounced an erosion of patriarchal power that allegedly left husbands ruined by their newly aggressive wives.

Romantic mythology miscasts the common colonists as self-sufficient yeomen, who produced all that they needed or wanted. In fact, every colonial farm produced crops for both household needs and the external market. By raising surplus crops for export, the colonists could pay for their imported consumer goods. Between 1720 and 1770 per capita colonial imports increased by 50 percent, and the aggregate value more than tripled from about £450,000 in 1700 to over £1,500,000 in 1750. In sum, the growing American market became critical to the profits and growth of British manufacturing.

During the mid-eighteenth century, widespread religious revivals also reflected the growing cultural integration of the transatlantic empire. Colonists had long sustained localized revivals of religious fervor in particular churches. During the 1730s, however, those revivals began to feed on each other in an accumulating series thanks to publications in London of influential reports from New Jersey and New England. In particular, Jonathan Edwards published *A Faithful Narrative* of his revivals in the Connecticut Valley. Widely read in Britain and the colonies, Edwards's account provided models of evangelical preaching and conversion that guided subsequent revivals. That influence gave a greater similarity to the revivals that the evangelicals then interpreted as a sure sign of God's uniform power.

The English readers of *A Faithful Narrative* included George Whitefield, a young Anglican minister who developed an innovative career as a tireless, itinerant evangelical, touring England and Wales, drawing thousands of listeners to open fields and parks. A masterful promoter, Whitefield exploited the marketing techniques of a commercial society, employing advance men, handbills, and newspaper notices to build his celebrity and his audiences. By crossing the Atlantic, Edwards's words had inspired Whitefield's preaching. In turn, the London newspapers passed in ships to the colonies to report Whitefield's sensational impact in England. News of his triumphs in London assured Whitefield of an eager audience among colonists who paid cultural deference to the great metropolis as the arbiter of all fashions.

In 1739–41, Whitefield toured the colonies from New England to Georgia. He drew huge crowds and reached even more colonists through his publications. His impact revealed the transatlantic integration of the British empire into a common market of shared goods and ideas. Along the way, in Philadelphia, he made a useful friend in Benjamin Franklin, the leading writer, publisher, and social reformer in the colonies. Although a confirmed rationalist who resisted Whitefield's evangelical message, Franklin admired Whitefield as a fellow entrepreneur and as a dazzling public performer. After Whitefield returned to England, his American supporters worked to sustain the momentum by leading many local revivals, collectively called a "Great Awakening."

But Whitefield also stirred controversy by blaming old-fashioned ministers for neglecting their duty to seek, experience, and preach evangelical conversion. Such rebukes divided the ministry, inspiring some to adopt his spontaneous, impassioned, evangelical style while others hardened in their opposition. The evangelicals became known as "New Lights," because they believed in new dispensations of divine grace, while their foes were "Old Lights," who defended venerable institutions and scriptural traditions. Used to a dispassionate style of worship, the Old Lights feared the outbursts evoked by the revivals: weeping, crying out, twitching, and falling down during worship. Most Old Light ministers were older men. Well established in their careers and set in their ways, they felt rattled by the ambitious zeal of New Light rivals, who tended to be younger and more adaptable to "new measures."

The revivals became even more controversial when they inspired some common people of little education and low status to become preachers who censored prestigious ministers as godless frauds. This was more than the well-educated Edwards and Whitefield had ever bargained on. By emphasizing the overwhelming miraculous and fundamental power of God acting directly and indiscriminately upon souls, the radical evangelicals weakened the social conventions of their hierarchical society. By insisting that every individual had a right to choose his or her own minister, the radicals championed individualism, a concept then considered divisive and anarchic. Free choice had radical implications for a colonial society, which insisted upon a social hierarchy, where husbands commanded wives, fathers dictated to sons, masters owned servants and slaves, and gentlemen claimed deference from common people. Although evangelicals insisted that they respected all claims to service and deference in the secular world, they argued that no worldly authority should obstruct religious choice.

Indeed, the radicals even preached to enslaved Africans, who responded positively to their accessible and emotional style of worship. Ordinarily reminded of their inferiority in every public encounter, the enslaved found in evangelical worship fleeting moments of equality with every other seeker. Many masters opposed the conversion of their slaves, lest it make them more defiant. To reassure them, the evangelicals insisted that they did not challenge slavery as an economic system. Instead, they prepared slaves for an afterlife where they would be, at last, free and equal—an eternity that seemed far more important than a lifetime endured in slavery.

The evangelical radicals promoted a more pluralistic, egalitarian, and voluntaristic social order by defending the free flow of itinerant preachers and their converts across community and denominational lines. The revivalists also imagined an enlarged society: an intercolonial and transatlantic network of congregations united by a shared spirituality communicated over long distances by itinerants and print. By no means did all colonists become evangelicals, but they were sufficiently numerous and interconnected to influence the entire culture.

Despite their ethnic and denominational diversity, the colonists and the British felt a new commonality as Protestants when they focused upon Catholic France, which had become the empire's greatest enemy. The British and their colonists despised their foils as economically backward, religiously superstitious, culturally decadent, and broken to despotic rule. By inverse definition, the British saw themselves as enlightened by commerce, individual liberties, the rule of law, and a Protestant faith. And they found their proof in the prosperity of the empire in both trade and war. Enthusiastic patriots of empire, the British colonists felt more strongly tied to the mother country—in contrast to the previous generation, when the Crown had threatened to reduce the colonies to abject dependence.

Chapter 8
Empires

Between 1689 and 1763, the British and the French waged four massive, imperial wars throughout the world's oceans and colonies as well as in Europe. The first war (1689–97) ended in a stalemate, but the second (1702–13) featured impressive English victories. In the peace treaty of 1713, the British secured Acadia (renamed Nova Scotia), Newfoundland, Hudson's Bay, and the West Indian island of St. Kitts. The third war (1738–48) proved inconsequential, but the British leaders decided to concentrate their forces in North America for the climactic fourth conflict (1754–63) known in Europe as "the Seven Years War" and in the British colonies as "the French and Indian War."

The British and the French came to blows over the vast and fertile Ohio Valley, just to the west of the Appalachian Mountains, which hemmed in the British colonists. In 1753–54 the French built Fort Duquesne at the forks of the Ohio River (present-day Pittsburgh) near a prime gateway through the mountains into the interior. In 1754, the British governor of Virginia sent a young and ambitious colonist, George Washington, with a regiment to drive the French out of Fort Duquesne. Inexperienced and rash, Washington bungled the expedition, making a premature attack that led to his humiliating surrender to the French and their native allies.

Casting Washington's defeat as French aggression, the British government made war in North America their highest priority, sending unprecedented numbers of troops across the Atlantic to seize control of the colonial frontier. In 1755, one combined force of British regulars and New English volunteers overwhelmed the French posts at the head of the Bay of Fundy in Nova Scotia. The victors then deported most of the Acadian French and confiscated their farms and livestock for appropriation by land speculators and settlers. But the primary British expedition reaped disaster in the woods of western Pennsylvania, when a veteran British general, Edward Braddock, marched 2,200 regular and colonial troops against Fort Duquesne. Brave but arrogant, Braddock led his men into an Indian ambush that destroyed his army. The dead included Braddock. The British debacle had one silver lining: George Washington inherited the command and redeemed his military reputation by ably conducting a retreat that saved half the army.

After Braddock's defeat, French-allied warriors ravaged the frontier settlements of Virginia, Maryland, and Pennsylvania. The raids pinned down colonial troops, which enabled the French to take the offensive in 1756 and 1757 under the able leadership of Governor-General Pierre de Rigaud de Vaudreuil and General Louis-Joseph de Montcalm, who captured British forts on Lake Ontario and Lake George.

In Great Britain, the embarrassing military setbacks brought to power a more competent administration headed by William Pitt, who invested even more troops and money in the North American fighting. Instead of ordering colonial cooperation, Pitt bought it by reimbursing in cash their expenditures, which dramatically increased the colonial contributions. Although politically expedient, Pitt's policy was financially reckless: by compounding the national debt, Pitt saddled the colonists and Britons with a burden that would later disrupt the empire. In 1758 in North America, the British employed some 45,000 troops, about half British regulars and half colonial volunteers—five times the

The brave old **Hendrick** the great S.ACHEM or Chief of the Mohawk Indians.
one of the Six Nations now in Alliance with & Subject to the King of Great Britain.
Sold by Eliz Bakewell opposite Birchin Lane in Cornhill.

11. The Mohawk leader Theyanoguin, known to the English as "Old
Hendrick," negotiated the peace in the French and Indian War. This
image reveals the cultural hybridity of the native leader, who traveled
to England to meet with Queen Anne, by combining native facial art
and props—a hatchet and wampum—with British clothing.

number of French troops in Canada. Never before had any empire spent so much money to wage war on a transoceanic scale.

The British war effort in North America also thrived as the Royal Navy won control of the Atlantic and devastated French shipping, reducing the reinforcements and supplies that reached New France. As trade goods became scarce at French posts, many Indians desperately sought an alternative supply of the guns, gunpowder, and shot needed for hunting and war. In the Ohio valley in 1758, as a new British army advanced on Fort Duquesne, the local natives deserted the French and reopened trade with the Pennsylvanians. Abandoned by their Indian allies, the French blew up their fort and fled northward.

In 1758–60, the British overwhelmed New France with sheer numbers of soldiers and sailors, warships, and cannon. In 1758 a massive British fleet and 13,000 regulars, commanded by General Jeffrey Amherst, captured the Fortress of Louisbourg near the mouth of the St. Lawrence River. A year later, General James Wolfe led a British army up the river to attack and capture Quebec— although both Montcalm and Wolfe died in the climactic battle. In 1760 Amherst completed the conquest by capturing Montreal, compelling Vaudreuil to surrender all of New France, including the forts around the Great Lakes to the west.

When the Spanish belatedly entered the war, they shared in the defeats inflicted on their French allies. The British captured the great Spanish port of Havana on the north shore of Cuba. In the western Pacific, another British fleet captured Manila, the capital of the Philippines, a Spanish colony. The British also secured a dominant position in India by routing the French and their local allies.

In early 1763 the belligerents made peace in the Treaty of Paris. The French conceded Canada and all of their claims east of the Mississippi, including the Ohio Valley, to the British. As a sop to appease their Spanish allies, the French gave them New Orleans and most of Louisiana (west of the Mississippi River). Although Louisiana was a troublesome money-loser as a colony, the Spanish hoped that it would enhance the security of New Spain as a frontier buffer zone. To regain Havana and Manila, the Spanish ceded Florida to the British. The Mississippi River became the new boundary between the British and the Spanish claims in North America. Of course, most of the interior remained in the possession of many Indian peoples, who denied that Europeans could dispose of their lands.

British success threatened the Indian peoples of the interior, for they had relied on playing off the rival empires against one another to maintain their own autonomy. With the French driven away, the British settlers could push inland, sweeping the Indians aside and transforming their land into farms and towns. And the British military commander, Jeffrey Amherst, foolishly cut off the delivery of presents expected by the Indians. He deemed presents a waste of money after the removal of the French competition.

Insulted and aggrieved, the Indians of the interior covertly prepared for war. The many diverse nations felt newly united by their shared grievances against the British traders, soldiers, and settlers. During the spring of 1763, far-flung native peoples surprised and captured most of the British forts around the Great Lakes and in the Ohio Valley. The British called this uprising "Pontiac's Rebellion," after an Ottawa chief prominent in the siege of Detroit. Although more influential than most chiefs, Pontiac could not command the diverse peoples dwelling in dozens of scattered villages. For their own shared reasons and under their own chiefs, many native peoples attacked the British posts and colonial settlements. The warriors hoped to lure the French back into North America, but they stayed in Europe. Although the allied Indians took many smaller forts around the Great Lakes, they failed to capture the three strongest British posts: Detroit, Niagara, and Fort Pitt.

The brutal war hardened animosities along racial lines. During the summer and fall of 1763, the warriors raided the settlements of western Pennsylvania, Maryland, and Virginia, killing or capturing about 2,000 colonists. Outraged by the atrocities of frontier war, the settlers treated all Indians, regardless of allegiance, as violent brutes best exterminated. In Pennsylvania, vigilantes, known as the "Paxton Boys," massacred the peaceful Indians of Conestoga. William Penn and his peaceful legacy were long dead in his colony.

By the summer of 1764, the British government sought to end the expensive and frustrating frontier war. Blaming Amherst for the crisis, the government recalled him and appointed a more flexible commander, Thomas Gage, who followed the pragmatic advice of the superintendent for Indian affairs, Sir William Johnson. Recognizing that presents and respect for Indians were far cheaper than military expeditions against them, Johnson adopted the French practices of the Middle Ground alliance. From 1764 to 1766 the various Indian peoples gradually made peace with Johnson, who distributed gifts with a lavish hand. Thereafter, British military officers practiced a new policy of conciliation at their western garrisons.

To further mollify the Indians, the Crown tried to enforce a new boundary line, which sought to keep settlers east of the Appalachian mountains and out of the Ohio Valley. But the 10,000 British soldiers scattered through North America could never enforce restraint on the dozens of cunning land speculators (including George Washington and Benjamin Franklin) and the thousands of determined settlers, who continued to flock westward into the Ohio Valley. British troops sometimes burned the log cabins of squatters, but these settlers soon returned in greater numbers to rebuild. Although ineffectual, the new boundary line irritated the colonists, who had expected the British to help them dispossess the Indians.

By conquering French Canada, the British unwittingly created a crisis within their own empire. The conquest deprived the colonists and the British of the common enemy that had united them in the past. Victory also invited the British to redefine the empire and to increase the colonists' burdens. But victory also emboldened the colonists to defy British demands with a new impunity because they no longer needed protection against the French.

Victory had not come cheap, doubling the British debt from a prewar £73 million to a postwar £137 million. After making such a major investment in North America, the British were not about to resume their former policy of benign neglect. During the 1760s, British officials concluded that the empire was too weak and the colonists too insubordinate. The British tightened enforcement of the trade laws, maintained a permanent garrison in North America, and imposed new taxes to fund the troops. Impressed by the apparent prosperity of the colonists, British insisted that they could indeed pay higher taxes to support the empire. This seemed only fair to the British, who had spent so much blood and treasure making the continent safe for the prospering colonists. And British taxpayers were already paying far heavier taxes than did the colonists.

But the shift in imperial policy shocked the colonial leaders, who devoutly believed that their prime right as Britons was to pay no taxes save those adopted by their own elected assemblies. The colonists dreaded that Parliamentary taxation would lead to a colonial poverty and dependence that they likened to "slavery." From their own practice on Africans, colonists knew where unchecked domination could ultimately lead. Slavery rendered liberty the more dear to the colonial owners of human property.

The increased British demands also coincided with a postwar depression in the colonial economy. Long troubled by a shortage of currency, the colonial economy had thrived during the war from the infusion of British money—but then suffered a depression when Parliament stopped the transfer payments at the end of the war. In the subsequent hard times of the mid-1760s, incomes fell and British creditors sued their colonial debtors. The new taxes and the stricter customs regulations came at an especially bad time for the colonists.

Rather than preserving the North American empire, the new postwar garrisons (and their associated taxes) provoked the crisis that lost most of that empire. The colonists concluded that the imperial army served to protect natives from settlers—rather than to help them dispossess the Indians.

When the civil war within the empire erupted in 1775–76, Nova Scotia, Newfoundland, and Québec remained loyal. Less populous and more marginal colonies to the north, they depended upon British protection and markets. Far to the south, the West Indian sugar planters felt too inhibited by their slave majority and too reliant upon the British market for sugar to consider rebellion. But in the thirteen colonies along the Atlantic Seaboard, the colonists felt a new confidence in their own power as they noted their growing population. Postwar immigration and continued natural increase pushed their numbers from 1.5 million in 1754 to 2.5 million by 1775. In their swelling population, colonial leaders detected an importance and maturity that deserved greater respect from Parliament. When denied that respect, many colonists felt a new capacity to reject British rule. And they longed to conquer and to develop the continent for their own purposes in defiance of the new British alliance with the Indians.

In that revolutionary conflict, the rebelling colonists found new allies in their old enemies: the French and, informally, the Spanish. Humiliated by their defeats during the last war, the French and Spanish had resolved to strike back and to restore the balance of power at their next opportunity. Learning from defeat, they rebuilt and reformed their armies and navies. In the American Revolutionary War, the French and the Spanish proved far leaner and meaner adversaries for the British. In addition, the Spanish Empire had grown substantially along the Pacific Coast of North America in a bid to restrict British expansion westward.

During the 1760s the officials of New Spain heard alarming rumors of Russian and British advances toward the northwest coast of North America. Vague in their knowledge of that vast region, the Spanish prematurely concluded that the Russians and British were closing in on California and would soon outflank New Mexico to attack precious Mexico. In fact, the British and Russians were fewer and farther away than the Spanish imagined. Far to the northwest in subarctic Alaska, a few dozen Russian traders were preoccupied with the commercial harvest of sea otter pelts in the Aleutian Islands with the coerced help of the Aleut people. Known as *promyshlenniki*, the Russian traders had followed in the wake of the voyage of discovery conducted by Vitus Bering from Siberia in 1741. As for the British, their Hudson's Bay Company had not yet tried to breach the Rocky Mountains to find the Pacific, and the Royal Navy had only just begun scientific voyages into the South Pacific. But, among imperial officials, fearful misunderstanding was more motivating than reassuring truth.

In 1768 the Spanish Crown ordered the colonization of the Alta California coast to secure the unguarded northwestern door to Mexico. About 300,000 natives dwelled in Alta California: an especially impressive number given that only a few practiced horticulture. Instead, they lived by a complex and seasonally shifting mix of hunting and gathering, which made the most of their abundant environment. Armed with bows and snares, the men pursued elk, deer, antelope, and rabbit. With weirs, nets, and spears, they trapped and killed salmon by the thousand during spring runs. Along the coast, the men also hunted for marine mammals along the beaches or built canoes to pursue and take them in the ocean. Native women accumulated most of the native diet by gathering and processing edible seeds, roots, nuts, mushrooms, berries, and acorns, which they rendered into cakes or porridge. In this vast and diverse region, the natives had subdivided into dozens of bands and tribes, which over time developed great linguistic differences. In 1768 Alta California hosted at least ninety languages, drawn from seven different language families.

Lacking Hispanics to colonize California, the viceroy of New Spain meant to turn the native Indians into Hispanics by reeducating them in missions. Although the Franciscan mission system was in decay and discredit in New Mexico and Texas, the Spanish hoped to revive it in California—a measure of their desperation.

Under the leadership of Fray Junipero Serra, a missionary, and Captain Gaspar de Portolá, a soldier, the colonization of California began during the spring of 1769. At San Diego Bay the Spanish founded a mission supported by a *presidio* garrisoned by soldiers. Later that summer Spanish troops probed north to found another mission-presidio complex at Monterey Bay, which became their headquarters in Alta California. By Serra's death in August 1784, Alta California had two agricultural towns (San Jose and Los Angeles), four *presidios*, and nine missions.

Although greatly outnumbered by the natives, the Hispanics possessed an intimidating monopoly on horses, guns, and a formal command structure. Subdivided into many bands, the California Indians lacked traditions of alliance and institutions of military coordination. Unable to concert an extensive resistance, their overt rebellions were few and quickly suppressed. The major exception came at the Yuma crossing of the Colorado River along a land route from Mexico. In July 1781, the local Quechan Indians rebelled and destroyed the Spanish outpost, killing fifty-five Hispanics, including all four priests. Chronically short of soldiers, the Spanish authorities dared not reestablish their destroyed villages at the Yuma crossing.

Briefly opened in 1774, the overland route to California closed down after the Quechan uprising of 1781. Where the opening had encouraged a temporary boom in Alta California, the closing stunted the colony's further growth. Isolation from Mexico sentenced Alta California to little more than a subsistence economy. Spanish manufactured goods were prohibitively expensive because imported via distant Mexico by the difficult maritime route—where adverse winds and currents slowed ships. That distance also discouraged exports of California's bulky produce, primarily livestock and grains. Unable profitably to ship their produce to Mexico, the colonists were limited to the local market provided by the small *presidio* garrisons. In 1790 Alta California had only 1,000 Hispanic colonists, stretched thin along a 500-mile coast from San Francisco to San Diego and scattered among thousands of Indians. For want of colonists, the colony continued to depend upon remaking the native inhabitants into Hispanics.

The Franciscan missionaries allured Indians with religious rituals and sacred objects—as well as metal goods, domesticated livestock, and new crops. And, as their shamans failed to cure the introduced diseases, natives turned to the Franciscans as an alternative source of healing magic. Foraging horses, cattle, mules, sheep, and pigs consumed the wild plants and seeds, including acorns, critical to the native diet. Hungry natives then turned to the missions in search of an alternative source of food. The number of mission Indians (called "neophytes") more than doubled, from about 2,000 in 1776 to 4,650 in 1784. But most of Alta California's Indians clung to life beyond the missions, in the interior.

The Spanish insisted that they benefited the Indians by introducing Hispanic civilization and the Roman Catholic faith. The demanding missionaries imposed their culture upon the neophytes, who had to learn the Spanish language, the Catholic faith, and agricultural labor, and practice celibacy before marriage and monogamy within it. The priests refused to accept any reconsideration, sending troops to retrieve neophytes who ran away.

In the close quarters of the missions, the neophytes were easy prey to infectious diseases and to syphilis, which inflicted infertility and stillbirths on Indian women. Running short on coastal Indians, in 1797 *presidio* commanders began to send troops into the Central Valley of California to capture potential neophytes. For a generation, the military sweeps and some new missions kept the neophyte numbers growing a bit faster than disease killed them. In 1821 when Spanish rule ended, the system had grown to twenty missions with over 21,000 neophytes.

Alta California remained the most marginal colony on the long, northern frontier of New Spain. New Mexico and Texas seemed prosperous and secure by comparison. During the nineteenth century, this Hispanic weakness would attract growing attention from covetous Anglo-Americans, who detected an economic potential in California that had eluded Hispanic exploitation. The newcomers came to exploit the commercial links around and across the Pacific that Captain James Cook had initiated on behalf of the British Empire during the 1760s and 1770s.

To Europeans, the Pacific Ocean long remained the most mysterious part of the temperate earth. On the other side of the planet, the Pacific was especially distant and hard to reach from Europe. During the colonial era, the only western access by sea came via the narrow, rocky, and stormy Strait of Magellan at the southern tip of South America. During the early sixteenth century, the Spanish mariner Ferdinand Magellan had discovered that western route into and across the Pacific to the Philippines. Following up on Magellan's discoveries, the Spanish established a colony at Manila, which traded across the Pacific with Mexico, employing the island of Guam as a midway base to resupply their passing ships with water and provisions. For nearly two centuries, Spanish hostility and secrecy discouraged other Europeans from venturing into the Pacific unknown, save for a few brief raids by pirates.

During the 1760s, the decline of Spanish naval power enabled the British and French to probe the Pacific Ocean in the name of science. Determined to collect information more empirically and systematically, their voyages of exploration brought along cartographers, astronomers, naturalists, and skilled draftsmen to study and depict the waters, skies, plants, animals, weather, and peoples of distant coasts and islands. The collection and publication of geographic and scientific information became essential to claim new lands. This new system sought to identify marketable commodities for commercial exploitation and to facilitate the pacification of island peoples as imperial subjects.

The British probes surged ahead under the able leadership of Captain James Cook. In 1768–71 and again in 1772–75, Cook systematically crisscrossed the South Pacific. The two voyages established Cook's reputation as the preeminent explorer of the eighteenth century. More methodical and thorough than any other mariner, Cook developed maps, charts, and journals of unprecedented precision, defining the Pacific in print for distant Europeans.

In 1776–79, for his third and final voyage, Cook probed the North Pacific in search of the fabled Northwest Passage around North America. Sailing northeast from Tahiti in January 1778, Cook came upon the Hawaiian Islands, a mid-oceanic and subtropical range of volcanic peaks. Located 2,700 miles beyond Tahiti and 2,400 miles southwest of California, the Hawaiian Islands were the most geographically isolated cluster in the Pacific. The eight major islands formed an arc, 350 miles long, anchored at the southeast by the largest, Hawaii. Many fertile and lush valleys intersected the rugged terrain of steep hills and lofty volcanoes.

The Hawaiian people were Polynesians: South Pacific islanders adept at building and navigating double-hulled canoes propelled by both paddles and sails. About 1,000 years ago, some especially daring and desperate Polynesians sailed far beyond Tahiti into the open ocean and were skilled and lucky enough to find the Hawaiian Islands, where they raised abundant crops of *taro* (a tuber), sweet potatoes, yams, breadfruit, bananas, and coconuts. They also kept chickens, dogs, and pigs—but they had neither horses nor cattle. The Hawaiians lived in many small villages and in houses composed of light wooden frames with grass-thatch walls and roofs to keep off the frequent rains. In 1778 each of the four major chiefdoms dominated a major island: Hawaii, Maui, Oahu, and Kauai. The head chiefs maintained a form of feudalism, assigning lands and their commoners to subordinate chiefs in return for tribute and assistance in war. The pride and rivalries of chiefs provoked frequent wars fought with stone-headed spears, daggers, and clubs. Seeking a new military edge, they longed to trade their produce and pork for the metal knives offered by Cook's mariners.

From Hawaii, Cook sailed along the northwest coast of North America in search of the Northwest Passage, a sea route to connect Europe with the trade riches of Asia. After landing on Vancouver Island, Cook sailed northeastward up the coast to Alaska, closing the cartographic gap between the Spanish coastal probes of California and the Russian investigation of Alaska. But he found no Northwest Passage through or around the continent.

Instead, in the Pacific Northwest, Cook found an elaborate native culture adapted to a mild and rainy climate abounding in timber, fish, sea otters, seals, and whales. Amply supported by fishing and marine hunting, the 200,000 rain-coast inhabitants had never needed to develop horticulture. Although divided into at least six language groups and hundreds of villages, the rain-coast peoples shared important cultural elements including complex social hierarchies, elaborate ceremonies, and a highly stylized art expressed in wood carving. Each village had multiple chiefs, but one enjoyed local preeminence for his superior achievements in war, trade, and gift-giving.

In return for nails, knives, and other metal goods, the British mariners purchased 1,500 sea otter pelts for about six pence apiece in English goods. A year later, en route homeward (via Hawaii, where Cook died in a skirmish with the natives), they stopped in China, where each pelt sold for tea, silks, and porcelain worth about £250 when taken on to England. Launched as science,

Cook's voyage evolved into commerce. Intrigued by the profits, British and American merchants followed up Cook's discoveries by sending ships to trade at Nootka Sound and in other rain-coast harbors. Formerly the rare experience of government-sponsored explorers, circumnavigation became a commercial commonplace by the late 1780s.

Both inbound to the Pacific Northwest and outbound to China, the trading ships stopped at the Hawaiian Islands for rest, repairs, and a resupply of water, wood, and provisions. The Hawaiian Islands became the nexus in an emerging market integration of the Pacific by European shipping and shippers, linking North America with China and Europe. The rival chiefs sought guns and gunpowder to secure an edge in their conflicts with one another. Between 1786 and 1810, Chief Kamehameha of Hawaii won the local arms race to become the dominant chief in the islands. A man of powerful build, restless intelligence, voracious ambition, and ruthless opportunism, Kamehameha exploited the newcomers and their technology for his own ends. Although confronted with new germs, livestock, weeds, weapons, and missionaries, the Hawaiians managed to mitigate the shocks, retaining control of their land until the end of the nineteenth century, when they succumbed to a new empire, the United States, which had succeeded the British as the dominant power in North America.

The new United States embraced the continental expansion that the British had unleashed only to regret during the 1760s. Unlike the British, the American leaders aggressively promoted western settlement. In western lands, the Americans meant to reproduce a society of family farmers, which they deemed essential to sustain a republic. That vision of white liberty depended upon the dispossession of native peoples. Thomas Jefferson aptly described the United States as an "empire of liberty," by and for the white citizenry. The new American empire liberated their enterprise at the expense of the Indians and Hispanics across the continent to the Pacific.

Far from ending with the American Revolution, colonialism persisted in North America but from a new base on the Atlantic seaboard. During the early nineteenth century, the Americans crossed their continent to invade the Pacific. They absorbed half of the Pacific rain-coast in 1846 (leaving the other half to British Canada), conquered California in 1846–48, purchased Russian Alaska in 1867, and subverted the Hawaiian monarchy in 1898. Ultimately, the Americans succeeded and exceeded the British as the predominant colonizers of North America.

Timeline

BP = Before Present; CE = Common Era

ca. 15,000 BP	Paleo-Indian migration from Siberia into North America begins
ca. 9,000 BP	Global warming transforms environment, leads to transition from Paleo-Indian to Archaic cultures
ca. 300 CE	Mesoamerican crops of maize, beans, and squash adopted in southwest and in the Mississippian watershed
ca. 1100 CE	Peak of Hohokam, Anasazi, and Mississippian cultures
ca. 1150–1250 CE	Crisis for the Hohokam, Anasazi, and Mississippian cultures
1492	Christopher Columbus crosses the Atlantic to the West Indies
1493	Columbus returns to Hispaniola to launch Spanish colonization
1518	Introduction of African slaves to Hispaniola
1519–21	Hernán Cortés conquers the Aztecs of Tenochtitlán
1519–22	Magellan expedition crosses the Pacific and circumnavigates the globe
1539–43	De Soto expedition ravages the American southeast

1540–42	Coronado expedition probes the American southwest
1565	Menéndez de Avilés destroys French Fort Caroline and founds Spanish San Agustín in Florida
1585	Ralegh founds the short-lived English colony at Roanoke
1598	Oñate founds Spanish colony of New Mexico
1607	English settle at Jamestown in the new colony of Virginia
1608	Spanish create the town of Santa Fe in New Mexico
1608	Samuel de Champlain founds the French settlement of Quebec
1609	Champlain leads allied Indian attack on the Haudenosaunee
1613–14	Pocahontas captured, converts to Christianity, and marries John Rolfe
1620	English Puritans found Plymouth in New England
1622	Virginia Algonkins rebel under Opechancanough
1630	Puritans found the town of Boston and the colony of Massachusetts
1632	English colony of Maryland founded at the head of Chesapeake Bay
1636–37	Pequot War in New England
1640s	The Haudenosaunee destroy the Huron villages and their Jesuit missions
1651–63	English Parliament adopts the Navigation Acts
1655	The Dutch conquer New Sweden on the Delaware River
1663	The French Crown takes control of New France
1664	The English seize the Dutch colony of New Netherland, which becomes New York
1670	English West Indians found Charles Town in the new colony of Carolina
1675–76	King Philip's War in New England

1676	Bacon's Rebellion in Virginia
1680	Pueblo Revolt destroys Spanish colony of New Mexico
1682	William Penn founds the English colony of Pennsylvania
1688–89	Glorious Revolution in England and her colonies
1692	Witchcraft trials in Salem, Massachusetts
1692–93	Spanish rule restored in New Mexico
1699	French found the colony of Louisiana
1701	Haudenosaunee make peace with the French and their Indian allies
1704–6	Carolina's Indian allies destroy the Spanish missions of Florida
1707	Union of Scotland and England to create Great Britain
1713	British acquire French Acadia, which they rename "Nova Scotia"
1712	Fox Wars begin in the Great Lakes country
1715	Yamasee rebellion in Carolina
1716–18	Spanish found missions and *presidios* in Texas
1720	Spanish expedition of Villasur routed by the Pawnee near the Platte River
1733	James Oglethorpe founds the British colony of Georgia
1737	Jonathan Edwards publishes *A Faithful Narrative of the Surprising Work of God*
1739	Stono Rebellion by slaves in Carolina
1739–41	George Whitefield's preaching tour of British America
1741	Russian traders begin to exploit the Aleutian Islands and the coast of Alaska
1751	British Crown takes command of Georgia and allows slavery
1754	Seven Years War begins in North America

Timeline

1755	Braddock's defeat near Fort Duquesne
1758	Comanche destroy the San Saba mission in Texas
1758	British capture Fort Duquesne
1759	British General James Wolfe dies capturing Quebec
1760	Sir Jeffrey Amherst completes British conquest of Canada
1763	Treaty of Paris transfers Canada and Florida to British rule, and most of Louisiana to the Spanish
1763	British Royal Proclamation restricts colonial settlement west of the Appalachian Mountains
1763–6	Pontiac's Rebellion by natives around the Great Lakes
1764	Massacre of peaceful Conestoga Indians by the Paxton Boys
1768–79	Captain James Cook explores the Pacific for the British Empire
1769	Spanish found missions and *presidios* in Alta California
1775–76	Revolution erupts within the mainland colonies of British America
1778–79	Cook discovers the Polynesian peoples of the Hawaiian Islands, but he dies fighting them
1781	Quechan uprising closes the land route from Mexico to Alta California
1783	British recognize American independence
1784	Russians colonize Kodiak Island, Alaska
1786–1810	Chief Kamehameha unites the Hawaiian Islands under his rule
1846	The United States acquires the Oregon Territory
1846–48	The United States conquers the southwest from Mexico
1867	The United States purchases Russian Alaska
1898	The United States seizes the Hawaiian Islands

Colonial America

Further reading

Introduction: Maps

For the Nasaw map, see Mark Warhus, *Another America: Native Maps and the History of Our Land* (New York: St. Martin's Press, 1997); Gregory A. Waselkov, "Indian Maps of the Colonial Southeast," in Peter H. Wood, Gregory A. Waselkov, and M. Thomas Hatley, eds., *Powhatan's Mantle: Indians in the Colonial Southeast* (Lincoln: University of Nebraska Press, 1989), 320–24.

For more detailed overviews of the colonial experience, see Alan Taylor, *American Colonies* (New York: Viking/Penguin, 2001); Gary B. Nash, *Red, White, and Black: The Peoples of Early America* (Upper Saddle River, NJ: Prentice-Hall, 2006); Daniel K. Richter, *Before the Revolution: America's Ancient Pasts* (Cambridge, MA: Harvard University Press, 2011); Richter, *Facing East from Indian Country: A Native History of Early America* (Cambridge, MA: Harvard University Press, 2001).

For native relations with empires, see Andrew R. L. Cayton and Fredrika J. Teute, eds., *Contact Points: American Frontiers from the Mohawk Valley to the Mississippi, 1750–1830* (Chapel Hill: University of North Carolina Press, 1998); Christine Daniels and Michael V. Kennedy, eds. *Negotiated Empires: Centers and Peripheries in the Americas, 1500–1820* (New York: Routledge, 2002).

For the historiography, see James Hijiya, "Why the West Is Lost," *William and Mary Quarterly*, 3rd ser. 51, no. 2 (1994): 276–92; Paul W. Mapp, "Atlantic History from Imperial, Continental, and Pacific Perspectives," *William and Mary Quarterly*, 3rd. ser. 63 (2006): 713–24; John M. Murrin, "Beneficiaries of Catastrophe: The English

Colonies in America," in Eric Foner, ed., *The New American History* (Philadelphia: Temple University Press, 1997), 3–30; Claudio Saunt, "Go West: Mapping Early American Historiography," *William and Mary Quarterly*, 3rd ser. 65 (2008): 745–78.

Chapter 1: Encounters

For Native America before 1492, see Alvin M. Josephy Jr., ed., *America in 1492: The World of the Indian Peoples Before the Arrival of Columbus* (New York: Alfred A. Knopf, 1992); Charles C. Mann, *1491: New Revelations of the Americas before Columbus* (New York: Alfred A. Knopf, 2005); Timothy R. Pauketat and Thomas E. Emerson, *Cahokia: Domination and Ideology in the Mississippian World* (Lincoln: University of Nebraska Press, 1997); Pauketat, *Ancient Cahokia and the Mississippians* (New York: Cambridge University Press, 2004); Neal Salisbury, "The Indians' Old World: Native Americans and the Coming of Europeans," *William and Mary Quarterly*, 3rd. ser. 53 (July 1996): 435–58; Bruce G. Trigger and Wilcomb E. Washburn, eds., *The Cambridge History of the Native Peoples of the Americas, Volume I: North America*, pt. 1 (New York: Cambridge University Press, 1996).

For the expansion of early modern Europe, see J. H. Elliott, *Imperial Spain, 1469–1716* (London: Edward Arnold, 1963); Elliott, *The Old World and the New, 1492–1650* (New York: Cambridge University Press, 1970); Bernard Lewis, *Cultures in Conflict: Christians, Muslims, and Jews in the Age of Discovery* (New York: Oxford University Press, 1995); J. H. Parry, *The Age of Reconnaissance* (Berkeley: University of California Press, 1981); Stuart B. Schwartz, ed., *Implicit Understandings: Observing, Reporting, and Reflecting on the Encounters Between Europeans and Other Peoples in the Early Modern Era* (New York: Cambridge University Press, 1994), 96–133; Philip D. Curtin, *The Rise and Fall of the Plantation Complex* (New York: Cambridge University Press, 1990); John Thornton, *Africa and Africans in the Making of the Atlantic World, 1400–1680* (New York: Cambridge University Press, 1992).

For Columbus and Hispaniola, see Stephen Greenblatt, *Marvelous Possessions: The Wonder of the New World* (Chicago: University of Chicago Press, 1991); William D. Phillips Jr. and Carla Rahn Phillips, *The Worlds of Christopher Columbus* (New York: Cambridge University Press, 1992); Charles Gibson, *Spain in America* (New York: HarperCollins, 1966).

For the post-Columbian transformation, see Alfred W. Crosby Jr., *Ecological Imperialism: The Biological Expansion of Europe, 900–1900* (New York: Cambridge University Press, 1986); Crosby, *The Columbian Exchange: Biological and Cultural Consequences of 1492* (Westport, CT: Greenwood Press, 1972); Jared Diamond, *Guns, Germs, and Steel: The Fates of Human Societies* (New York: W. W. Norton, 1998); Elinor G. K. Melville, *A Plague of Sheep: Environmental Consequences of the Conquest of Mexico* (New York: Cambridge University Press, 1994); Colin G. Calloway, *New Worlds for All: Indians, Europeans, and the Remaking of Early America* (Baltimore: Johns Hopkins University Press, 1997).

For the population history of North America, see John D. Daniels, "The Indian Population of North America in 1492," *William and Mary Quarterly*, 3rd ser. 49 (April 1992): 298–320; Kenneth F. Kiple and Stephen V. Beck, eds., *Biological Consequences of the European Expansion, 1450–1800* (Brookfield, VT: Ashgate/Variorum, 1997); Kenneth F. Kiple, ed., *The Cambridge World History of Human Disease* (New York: Cambridge University Press, 1993); William H. McNeill, *Plagues and Peoples* (New York: Anchor Press, 1976); John W. Verano and Douglas H. Ubelaker, eds., *Disease and Demography in the Americas* (Washington, DC: Smithsonian Institution Press, 1992).

Chapter 2: New Spain

For the Spanish conquests, see Inga Clendinnen, *Aztecs: An Interpretation* (New York: Cambridge University Press, 1993); Leslie Bethell, ed., *Colonial Spanish America* (New York: Cambridge University Press, 1987), 1–58; J. H. Parry, *The Age of Reconnaissance* (Berkeley: University of California Press, 1981).

For the consolidation of New Spain, see Richard L. Kagan and Geoffrey Parker, eds., *Spain, Europe and the Atlantic World: Essays in Honour of John H. Elliott* (New York: Cambridge University Press, 1995); J. H. Elliott, *Spain and Its World, 1500–1700: Selected Essays* (New Haven, CT: Yale University Press, 1989); James Lockhart and Stuart B. Schwartz, *Early Latin America: A History of Colonial Spanish America and Brazil* (New York: Cambridge University Press, 1983); John Lynch, *Spain, 1516–1598: From Nation State to World Empire* (Oxford: Blackwell, 1992).

For emigration to New Spain, see Ida Altman and James Horn, eds., *"To Make America": European Emigration in the Early Modern Period* (Berkeley: University of California Press, 1991); Nicholas Canny, ed.,

Europeans on the Move: Studies on European Migration, 1500–1800
(Oxford: Oxford University Press, 1994), 26–36.

For the Spanish expansion into the American Southeast and
Southwest, see Robert C. Galgano, *Feast of Souls: Indians and
Spaniards in the Seventeenth-Century Missions of Florida and New
Mexico* (Albuquerque: University of New Mexico Press, 2005); Charles
Hudson and Carmen Chaves Tesser, eds., *The Forgotten Centuries:
Indians and Europeans in the American South, 1521–1704* (Athens:
University of Georgia Press, 1994), 36–49, 50–73; Andres Resendez, *A
Land So Strange: The Epic Journey of Cabeza de Vaca* (New York: Basic
Books, 2007); David J. Weber, *The Spanish Frontier in North America*
(New Haven, CT: Yale University Press, 1992).

For native resistance in New Mexico, see James F. Brooks, *Captives
and Cousins: Slavery, Kinship, and Community in the Southwest
Borderlands* (Chapel Hill: University of North Carolina Press, 2002);
Jack D. Forbes, *Apache, Navaho, and Spaniard* (Norman: University of
Oklahoma Press, 1994); Elizabeth A. H. John, *Storms Brewed in Other
Men's Worlds: The Confrontation of Indians, Spanish, and French in
the Southwest, 1540–1795* (Norman: University of Oklahoma Press,
1996); Andrew L. Knaut, *The Pueblo Revolt of 1680: Conquest and
Resistance in Seventeenth-Century New Mexico* (Norman: University
of Oklahoma Press, 1997); David J. Weber, *Barbaros: Spaniards and
Their Savages in the Age of Enlightenment* (New Haven, CT: Yale
University Press, 2005).

Chapter 3: New France

For French Canada and its native peoples, see Denys Delage, *Bitter
Feast: Amerindians and Europeans in Northeastern North America,
1600–1664*, trans. Jane Brierly (Vancouver: UBC Press, 1993); Olive
Patricia Dickason, *Canada's First Nations: A History of Founding
Peoples from Earliest Times* (Norman: University of Oklahoma Press,
1992); W. J. Eccles, *France in America* (East Lansing: Michigan State
University Press, 1990); Bruce G. Trigger, *Natives and Newcomers:
Canada's "Heroic Age" Reconsidered* (Montreal: McGill-Queen's
University Press, 1986).

For the early fur trade, see James Axtell, *After Columbus: Essays in the
Ethnohistory of Colonial North America* (New York: Oxford University
Press, 1988), 144–81; Colin G. Calloway, ed., *Dawnland Encounters:
Indians and Europeans in Northern New England* (Hanover, NH:
University Press of New England, 1991); William Cronon, *Changes in*

the Land: Indians, Colonists, and the Ecology of New England (New York: Hill and Wang, 1983).

For the Haudenosaunee and the French, see James Axtell, *The Invasion Within: The Contest of Cultures in Colonial North America* (New York: Oxford University Press, 1985); Jose Antonio Brandao, *"Your Fyre Shall Burn No More": Iroquois Policy toward New France and Its Native Allies to 1701* (Lincoln: University of Nebraska Press, 1997); Matthew Dennis, *Cultivating a Landscape of Peace: Iroquois-European Encounters in Seventeenth-Century America* (Ithaca, NY: Cornell University Press, 1993); Daniel K. Richter, *The Ordeal of the Longhouse: The Peoples of the Iroquois League in the Era of European Colonization* (Chapel Hill: University of North Carolina Press, 1992); Dean R. Snow, *The Iroquois* (Cambridge, MA: Harvard University Press, 1994); Ian K. Steele, *Warpaths: Invasions of North America* (New York: Oxford University Press, 1994).

For the settlement of New France, see W. J. Eccles, *Essays on New France* (Toronto: Oxford University Press, 1987); Allan Greer, *The People of New France* (Toronto: University of Toronto Press, 1997); Greer, *Mohawk Saint: Catherine Tekakwitha and the Jesuits* (New York: Oxford University Press, 2005); Jan Noel, *Women in New France* (Ottawa: Canadian Historical Association, 1998); Peter Moogk, *La Nouvelle France: The Making of French Canada, a Cultural History* (East Lansing: Michigan State University Press, 2000).

For the Middle Ground, see Kathleen Duval, *The Native Ground: Indians and Colonists in the Heart of the Continent* (Philadelphia: University of Pennsylvania Press, 2006); Eric Hinderaker, *Elusive Empires: Constructing Colonialism in the Ohio Valley, 1673–1800* (New York: Cambridge University Press, 1997); Susan Sleeper-Smith, *Indian Women and French Men: Rethinking Cultural Encounter in the Western Great Lakes* (Amherst: University of Massachusetts Press, 2001); Richard White, *The Middle Ground: Indians, Empires, and Republics in the Great Lakes Region, 1650–1815* (New York: Cambridge University Press, 1991).

For Louisiana, see Patricia K. Galloway, ed., *La Salle and His Legacy: Frenchmen and Indians in the Lower Mississippi Valley* (Jackson: University Press of Mississippi, 1982); Gwendolyn Midlo Hall, *Africans in Colonial Louisiana: The Development of Afro-Creole Culture in the Eighteenth Century* (Baton Rouge: Louisiana State University Press, 1995); Daniel H. Usner Jr., *Indians, Settlers, and Slaves In a Frontier Exchange Economy: The Lower Mississippi Valley Before 1783* (Chapel Hill: University of North Carolina Press, 1992);

Patricia Dillon Woods, *French-Indian Relations on the Southern Frontier, 1699–1762* (Ann Arbor: University of Michigan Press, 1980).

For Indians in the Southeast, see Kathryn E. Holland Braund, *Deerskins and Duffels: The Creek Indian Trade with Anglo-America, 1685–1815* (Lincoln: University of Nebraska Press, 1993); Andrew R. L. Cayton and Fredrika J. Teute, eds., *Contact Points: American Frontiers from the Mohawk Valley to the Mississippi, 1750–1830* (Chapel Hill: University of North Carolina Press, 1998); James H. Merrell, *The Indians' New World: Catawbas and Their Neighbors from European Contact through the Era of Removal* (Chapel Hill: University of North Carolina Press, 1989); Richard White, *The Roots of Dependency: Subsistence, Environment, and Social Change among the Choctaws, Pawnees, and Navajos* (Lincoln: University of Nebraska Press, 1983); Peter H. Wood, Gregory A. Waselkov, and M. Thomas Hatley, eds., *Powhatan's Mantle: Indians in the Colonial Southeast* (Lincoln: University of Nebraska Press, 1989).

For Texas, the Great Basin, and the Great Plains, see Juliana Barr, *Peace Came in the Form of a Woman: Indians and Spaniards in the Texas Borderlands* (Chapel Hill: University of North Carolina Press, 2007); Ned Blackhawk, *Violence over the Land: Indians and Empires in the Early American West* (Cambridge, MA: Harvard University Press, 2006); Colin G. Calloway, *One Vast Winter Count: The Native American West before Lewis and Clark* (Lincoln: University of Nebraska Press, 2003); Elizabeth Anne Fenn, *Pox Americana: The Great Smallpox Epidemic of 1775–1782* (New York: Hill and Wang, 2001); Pekka Hamalainen. *The Comanche Empire* (New Haven, CT: Yale University Press, 2008).

Chapter 4: Chesapeake

For overviews of the colonial Chesapeake, see Warren M. Billings, John E. Selby, and Thad W. Tate, *Colonial Virginia: A History* (White Plains, NY: KTO Press, 1986); James Horn, *Adapting to a New World: English Society in the Seventeenth-Century Chesapeake* (Chapel Hill: University of North Carolina Press, 1994); Peter C. Mancall, ed., *The Atlantic World and Virginia, 1550–1624* (Chapel Hill: University of North Carolina Press, 2007); Edmund S. Morgan, *American Slavery, American Freedom: The Ordeal of Colonial Virginia* (New York: W. W. Norton, 1975).

For the English and Irish origins of Chesapeake colonization, see K. R. Andrews, N. P. Canny, and P. E. H. Hair, eds., *The Westward*

Enterprise: English Activities in Ireland, the Atlantic, and America, 1480–1650 (Detroit: Wayne State University press, 1979); Nicholas P. Canny, "The Ideology of English Colonization: From Ireland to America," *William and Mary Quarterly*, 3rd. ser. 30 (1973): 575–98; Canny, ed., *The Oxford History of the British Empire: Volume I: The Origins of Empire, British Overseas Enterprise to the Close of the Seventeenth Century* (Oxford: Oxford University Press, 1998); Allison Games, *The Web of Empire: English Cosmopolitans in an Age of Expansion, 1560–1660* (New York: Oxford University Press, 2008); Mark Kishlansky, *A Monarchy Transformed: Britain, 1603–1714* (New York: Penguin, 1996); Peter C. Mancall, ed., *Envisioning America: English Plans for the Colonization of North America, 1580–1640* (New York: Bedford Books of St. Martin's Press, 1995); David B. Quinn, *North America From Earliest Discovery to First Settlements: The Norse Voyages to 1612* (New York: Harper and Row, 1977).

For the Powhatan Indians, see Frederick W. Gleach, *Powhatan's World and Colonial Virginia: A Conflict of Cultures* (Lincoln: University of Nebraska Press, 1997); Charles Hudson and Carmen Chaves Tesser, eds., *The Forgotten Centuries: Indians and Europeans in the American South, 1521–1704* (Athens: University of Georgia Press, 1994); Helen C. Rountree, *Pocahontas's People: The Powhatan Indians of Virginia Through Four Centuries* (Norman: University of Oklahoma Press, 1990); Rountree, *Pocahontas, Powhatan, Opechancanough: Three Indian Lives Changed by Jamestown* (Charlottesville: University Press of Virginia, 2005); Margaret Holmes Williamson, *Powhatan Lords of Life and Death: Command and Consent in Seventeenth-Century Virginia* (Lincoln: University of Nebraska Press, 2003).

For the first colonies, see Kenneth R. Andrews, *Trade, Plunder, and Settlement: Maritime Enterprise and the Genesis of the British Empire, 1480–1630* (New York: Cambridge University Press, 1984); Karen Ordahl Kupperman, *Roanoke: The Abandoned Colony* (Totowa, NJ: Rowman and Allanheld, 1984); Thad W. Tate and David L. Ammerman, eds., *The Chesapeake in the Seventeenth Century: Essays on Anglo-American Society* (Chapel Hill: University of North Carolina Press, 1979).

For colonial Virginia and Maryland, see Bernard Bailyn, "Politics and Social Structure in Virginia," in James Morton Smith, ed., *Seventeenth-Century America: Essays in Colonial History* (Chapel Hill: University of North Carolina Press, 1959); Kathleen M. Brown, *Good Wives, Nasty Wenches, and Anxious Patriarchs: Gender, Race,* and *Power in Colonial Virginia* (Chapel Hill: University of North Carolina Press, 1996); Lois Green Carr, Russell R. Menard, and Lorena S. Walsh, *Robert Cole's World: Agriculture and Society in Early Maryland* (Chapel Hill: University of North Carolina Press, 1991); Lois Green Carr, Philip D. Morgan, and Jean B. Russo, eds., *Colonial Chesapeake Society* (Chapel Hill: University of North Carolina Press, 1988); Gloria L. Main, *Tobacco Colony: Life in Early Maryland, 1650–1720* (Princeton, NJ: Princeton University Press, 1982); Mary Beth Norton, *Founding Mothers and Fathers: Gendered Power and the Forming of American Society* (New York: Alfred A. Knopf, 1996).

For Virginia's transition to slavery, see Ira Berlin, *Many Thousands Gone: The First Two Centuries of Slavery in North America* (Cambridge, MA: Harvard University Press, 1998); T. H. Breen and Stephen Innes, *"Myne Owne Ground": Race and Freedom on Virginia's Eastern Shore, 1640–1676* (New York: Oxford University Press, 1980); Winthrop D. Jordan, *White over Black: American Attitudes Toward the Negro, 1550–1812* (New York: Oxford University Press, 1977); Anthony S. Parent Jr., *Foul Means: The Formation of a Slave Society in Virginia, 1660–1740* (Chapel Hill: University of North Carolina Press, 2003).

Chapter 5: New England

For England and Puritanism, see Patrick Collinson, *The Birthpangs of Protestant England: Religious and Cultural Change in the Sixteenth and Seventeenth Centuries* (London: Macmillan, 1988); Collinson, *The Religion of Protestants: The Church in English Society, 1559–1625* (Oxford: Clarendon Press, 1982); Mark Kishlansky, *A Monarchy Transformed: Britain, 1603–1714* (New York: Penguin, 1996).

For Puritanism in New England, see Theodore Dwight Bozeman, *To Live Ancient Lives: The Primitivist Dimension in Puritanism* (Chapel Hill: University of North Carolina Press, 1988); Charles Lloyd Cohen, *God's Caress: The Psychology of Puritan Religious Experience* (New York: Oxford University Press, 1986); Stephen Foster, *The Long Argument: English Puritanism and the Shaping of New England Culture, 1570–1700* (Chapel Hill: University of North Carolina Press, 1991); David D. Hall, *Worlds of Wonder, Days of Judgment: Popular Religious Belief in Early New England* (New York: Alfred A. Knopf, 1989).

For immigration to New England, see Virginia DeJohn Anderson, *New England's Generation: The Great Migration and the Formation of*

Society and Culture in the Seventeenth Century (New York: Cambridge University Press, 1991); David Cressy, *Coming Over: Migration and Communication between England and New England in the Seventeenth Century* (New York: Cambridge University Press, 1987).

For the colonies of New England, see Charles E. Clark, *The Eastern Frontier: The Settlement of Northern New England, 1610–1763* (New York: Alfred A. Knopf, 1970); Bruce C. Daniels, *The Connecticut Town: Growth and Development, 1635–1790* (Middletown, CT: Wesleyan University Press, 1979); Daniels, *Dissent and Conformity on Narragansett Bay: The Colonial Rhode Island Town* (Middletown, CT: Wesleyan University Press, 1983); John Demos, *A Little Commonwealth: Family Life in Plymouth Colony* (New York: Oxford University Press, 1970).

For the Indians of New England, see Kathleen J. Bragdon, *Native People of Southern New England, 1500–1650* (Norman: University of Oklahoma Press, 1996); Jenny Hale Pulsipher, *Subjects unto the Same King: Indians, English, and the Contest for Authority in Colonial New England* (Philadelphia: University of Pennsylvania Press, 2005); William S. Simmons, *Spirit of the New England Tribes: Indian History and Folklore, 1620–1984* (Hanover, NH: University Press of New England, 1986).

For Indian-Puritan relations, see James Axtell, *The Invasion Within: The Contest of Cultures in Colonial North America* (New York: Oxford University Press, 1985); Colin G. Calloway, ed., *After King Philip's War: Presence and Persistence in Indian New England* (Hanover, NH: University Press of New England, 1997); Jill Lepore, *The Name of War: King Philip's War and the Origins of American Identity* (New York: Alfred A. Knopf, 1998); Jean M. O'Brien, *Dispossession by Degrees: Indian Land and Identity in Natick, Massachusetts, 1650–1790* (New York: Cambridge University Press, 1997); Neal Salisbury, *Manitou and Providence: Indians, Europeans, and the Making of New England, 1500–1643* (New York: Oxford University Press, 1982); David J. Silverman, *Faith and Boundaries: Colonists, Christianity, and Community among the Wampanoag Indians of Martha's Vineyard, 1600–1871* (New York: Cambridge University Press, 2005); Ian K. Steele, *Warpaths: Invasions of North America* (New York: Oxford University Press, 1994).

For women's experience, see Cornelia Hughes Dayton, *Women Before the Bar: Gender, Law, and Society in Connecticut, 1639–1789* (Chapel Hill: University of North Carolina Press, 1995); Mary Beth Norton, *Founding Mothers and Fathers: Gendered Power and the Forming of*

American Society (New York: Alfred A. Knopf, 1996); Laurel Thatcher Ulrich, *Good Wives: Image and Reality in the Lives of Women in Northern New England, 1650-1750* (New York: Alfred A. Knopf, 1982).

For witchcraft, see Paul Boyer and Stephen Nissenbaum, *Salem Possessed: The Social Origins of Witchcraft* (Cambridge, MA: Harvard University Press, 1974); John P. Demos, *Entertaining Satan: Witchcraft and the Culture of Early New England* (New York: Oxford University Press, 1982); Carol F. Karlsen, *The Devil in the Shape of a Woman: Witchcraft in Colonial New England* (New York: W. W. Norton, 1987).

For the environmental and economic transformation of New England, see William Cronon, *Changes in the Land: Indians, Colonists, and the Ecology of New England* (New York: Hill and Wang, 1983); Christine Leigh Heyrman, *Commerce and Culture: The Maritime Communities of Colonial Massachusetts, 1690-1750* (New York: W. W. Norton, 1984); Stephen Innes, *Creating the Commonwealth: The Economic Culture of Puritan New England* (New York: W. W. Norton, 1995); John J. McCusker and Russell R. Menard, *The Economy of British America, 1607-1789* (Chapel Hill: University of North Carolina Press, 1985); Daniel Vickers, *Farmers and Fishermen: Two Centuries of Work in Essex County, Massachusetts, 1630-1850* (Chapel Hill: University of North Carolina Press, 1994).

Chapter 6: West Indies and Carolina

For the West Indies, see Hilary McD. Beckles, *White Servitude and Black Slavery in Barbados, 1627-1715* (Knoxville: University of Tennessee Press, 1989); Barbara Bush, *Slave Women in Caribbean Society, 1650-1838* (Bloomington: University of Indiana Press, 1990); Philip D. Curtin, *The Rise and Fall of the Plantation Complex: Essays in Atlantic History* (New York: Cambridge University Press, 1998); Richard S. Dunn, *Sugar and Slaves: The Rise of the Planter Class in the English West Indies, 1624-1713* (Chapel Hill: University of North Carolina Press, 1972); John J. McCusker and Russell R. Menard, *The Economy of British America, 1607-1789* (Chapel Hill: University of North Carolina Press, 1985); Richard B. Sheridan, *Sugar and Slavery: An Economic History of the British West Indies, 1623-1775* (Baltimore: Johns Hopkins University Press, 1973).

For early Carolina, see Daniel C. Littlefield, *Rice and Slaves: Ethnicity and the Slave Trade in Colonial South Carolina* (Baton Rouge: Louisiana State University Press, 1981); Peter H. Wood, *Black*

Majority: Negroes in Colonial South Carolina from 1670 through the Stono Rebellion (New York: Alfred A. Knopf, 1974); Peter H. Wood, Gregory A. Waselkov, and M. Thomas Hatley, eds., *Powhatan's Mantle: Indians in the Colonial Southeast* (Lincoln: University of Nebraska Press, 1989).

For the development of the Carolina deerskin and slave trades, see James Axtell, *The Indians' New South: Cultural Change in the Colonial Southeast* (Baton Rouge: Louisiana State University Press, 1997); Allan Gallay, *The Indian Slave Trade: The Rise of the English Empire in the American South, 1670-1717* (New Haven, CT: Yale University Press, 2002); James H. Merrell, *The Indians' New World: Catawbas and Their Neighbors from European Contact through the Era of Removal* (Chapel Hill: University of North Carolina Press, 1989); Joshua Piker, *Okfuskee: A Creek Indian Town in Colonial America* (Cambridge, MA: Harvard University Press, 2004).

For early Georgia, see Harvey H. Jackson and Phinizy Spalding, eds., *Forty Years of Diversity: Essays on Colonial Georgia* (Athens: University of Georgia Press, 1984); Jackson and Spalding, eds., *Oglethorpe in Perspective: Georgia's Founder after Two Hundred Years* (Tuscaloosa: University of Alabama Press, 1989); Betty Wood, *Slavery in Colonial Georgia, 1730-1775* (Athens: University of Georgia Press, 1984).

Chapter 7: British America

For the Dutch empire, see Jonathan I. Israel, *The Dutch Republic: Its Rise, Greatness, and Fall, 1477-1806* (New York: Oxford University Press, 1998); J. L. Price, *The Dutch Republic in the Seventeenth Century* (New York: St. Martin's Press, 1998).

For New Netherland, see Patricia U. Bonomi and Eric Nooter, eds., *Colonial Dutch Studies: An Interdisciplinary Approach* (New York: New York University Press, 1988); Jaap Jacobs, *The Colony of New Netherland: A Dutch Settlement in Seventeenth-Century America* (Ithaca, NY: Cornell University Press, 2009); David E. Narrett, *Inheritance and Family Life in Colonial New York City* (Ithaca, NY: Cornell University Press, 1992); William Pencak and Conrad Edick Wright, eds., *Authority and Resistance in Early New York* (New York: New-York Historical Society, 1988); Oliver A. Rink, *Holland on the Hudson: An Economic and Social History of Dutch New York* (Ithaca, NY: Cornell University Press, 1986).

For the English empire in the seventeenth century, see Robert M. Bliss, *Revolution and Empire: English Politics and the American*

Colonies in the Seventeenth Century (New York: Manchester University Press, 1990); Nicholas Canny and Alaine Low, eds., *The Origins of Empire: British Overseas Enterprise to the Close of the Seventeenth Century* (Oxford: Oxford University Press, 1998); Carla Gardina Pestana, *The English Atlantic in an Age of Revolution, 1640–1661* (Cambridge, MA: Harvard University Press, 2004).

For the transfer of New Netherland to New York, see Randall Balmer, *A Perfect Babel of Confusion: Dutch Religion and English Culture in the Middle Colonies* (New York: Oxford University Press, 1989); Joyce D. Goodfriend, *Before the Melting Pot: Society and Culture in Colonial New York City, 1664–1730* (Princeton, NJ: Princeton University Press, 1992); Donna Merwick, *Possessing Albany, 1630–1710: The Dutch and English Experiences* (New York: Cambridge University Press, 1990); Robert C. Ritchie, *The Duke's Province: A Study of New York Politics and Society, 1664–1691* (Chapel Hill: University of North Carolina Press, 1977).

For New Jersey and Pennsylvania, see Mary Maples Dunn, *William Penn, Politics and Conscience* (Princeton, NJ: Princeton University Press, 1967); Richard S. Dunn and Mary Maples Dunn, eds., *The World of William Penn* (Philadelphia: University of Pennsylvania Press, 1986); Ned C. Landsman, *Scotland and its First American Colony, 1683–1765* (Princeton, NJ: Princeton University Press, 1985); Gary B. Nash, *Quakers and Politics: Pennsylvania, 1681–1726* (Princeton, NJ: Princeton University Press, 1968); Sally Schwartz, *"A Mixed Multitude": The Struggle for Toleration in Colonial Pennsylvania* (New York: New York University Press, 1988).

For the Dominion, see T. H. Breen, *The Character of the Good Ruler: A Study of Puritan Political Ideas in New England, 1630–1730* (New Haven, CT: Yale University Press, 1970); Michael G. Hall, *Edward Randolph and the American Colonies, 1676–1703* (Chapel Hill: University of North Carolina Press, 1960); Richard R. Johnson, *Adjustment to Empire: The New England Colonies, 1675–1715* (New Brunswick, NJ: Rutgers University Press, 1981).

For the Glorious Revolution, see Robert Beddard, ed., *The Revolutions of 1688* (Oxford: Clarendon Press, 1991); Nicholas Canny and Alaine Low, eds., *The Origins of Empire: British Overseas Enterprise to the Close of the Seventeenth Century* (Oxford: Oxford University Press, 1998), 445–66; Jonathan I. Israel, ed., *The Anglo-Dutch Moment: Essays on the Glorious Revolution and its World Impact* (New York: Cambridge University Press, 1991); Steve Pincus, *1688: The First Modern Revolution* (New Haven, CT: Yale University

Press, 2009); Jack M. Sosin, *English America and the Revolution of 1688* (Lincoln: University of Nebraska Press, 1982).

For the impact of the Glorious Revolution in the colonies, see Patricia U. Bonomi, *The Lord Cornbury Scandal: The Politics of Reputation in British America* (Chapel Hill: University of North Carolina Press, 1998); Richard L. Bushman, *King and People in Provincial Massachusetts* (Chapel Hill: University of North Carolina Press, 1985); Edmund S. Morgan, *Inventing the People: The Rise of Popular Sovereignty in England and America* (New York: W. W. Norton, 1988).

For the development of the fiscal-military state and the British Union, see Jeremy Black, *Britain as a Military Power, 1688–1815* (London: University College London Press, 1999); Jeremy Black and Philip Woodfine, eds., *The British Navy and the Use of Naval Power in the Eighteenth Century* (Leicester: Leicester University Press, 1988); John Brewer, *The Sinews of Power: War, Money, and the English State, 1688–1783* (New York: Alfred A. Knopf, 1989); Mark Kishlansky, *A Monarchy Transformed: Britain, 1603–1714* (New York: Penguin, 1996); P. J. Marshall, ed., *The Oxford History of the British Empire, Volume II: The Eighteenth Century* (Oxford: Oxford University Press, 1998); Lawrence Stone, ed., *An Imperial State at War: Britain from 1689 to 1815* (New York: Routledge, 1994).

For the commercial empire, see Linda Colley, *Britons: Forging the Nation, 1707–1837* (New Haven, CT: Yale University Press, 1992); Stanley L. Engerman and Robert E. Gallman, eds., *The Cambridge Economic History of the United States*, vol. 1, *The Colonial Era* (New York: Cambridge University Press, 1996), 337–62; John J. McCusker and Russell R. Menard, *The Economy of British America, 1607–1789* (Chapel Hill: University of North Carolina Press, 1985); Ian K. Steele, *The English Atlantic, 1675–1740: An Exploration of Communication and Community* (New York: Oxford University Press, 1986).

For gentility and the consumer revolution, see T. H. Breen, *The Marketplace of Revolution: How Consumer Politics Shaped American Independence* (New York: Oxford University Press, 2004); Richard Bushman, *The Refinement of America: Persons, Houses, Cities* (New York: Alfred A. Knopf, 1992); Cary Carson, Ronald Hoffman, and Peter J. Albert, eds., *Of Consuming Interests: The Style of Life in the Eighteenth Century* (Charlottesville: University Press of Virginia, 1994).

For eighteenth-century colonial immigration, see Marilyn C. Baseler, *"Asylum for Mankind": America, 1607–1800* (Ithaca, NY: Cornell

University Press, 1998); Bernard Bailyn, *Voyagers to the West: A Passage in the Peopling of America on the Eve of the Revolution* (New York: Alfred A. Knopf, 1986); Bernard Bailyn and Philip D. Morgan, eds., *Strangers within the Realm: Cultural Margins of the First British Empire* (Chapel Hill: University of North Carolina Press, 1991); Nicholas Canny, ed., *Europeans on the Move: Studies on European Migration, 1500–1800* (New York: Oxford University Press, 1994); Aaron Spencer Fogleman, *Hopeful Journeys: German Immigration, Settlement, and Political Culture in Colonial America, 1717–1775* (Philadelphia: University of Pennsylvania Press, 1996); Patrick Griffin, *The People with No Name: Ireland's Ulster Scots, America's Scots Irish, and the Creation of a British Atlantic World, 1689–1764* (Princeton, NJ: Princeton University Press, 2001); Marianne Wokeck, *Trade in Strangers: The Beginnings of Mass Migration to North America* (University Park: Pennsylvania State University Press, 1999).

For slavery and the slave trade, see Ira Berlin, *Many Thousands Gone: The First Two Centuries of Slavery in North America* (Cambridge, MA: Harvard University Press, 1998); Robin Blackburn, *The Making of New World Slavery: From the Baroque to the Modern, 1492–1800* (New York: Verso, 1997); Herbert S. Klein, *The Atlantic Slave Trade* (New York: Cambridge University Press, 1999); Allan Kulikoff, *Tobacco and Slaves: The Development of Southern Cultures in the Chesapeake, 1660–1800* (Chapel Hill: University of North Carolina Press, 1986); Philip D. Morgan, *Slave Counterpoint: Black Culture in the Eighteenth-Century Chesapeake and Lowcountry* (Chapel Hill: University of North Carolina Press, 1998); John Thornton, *Africa and Africans in the Making of the Atlantic World, 1400–1680* (New York: Cambridge University Press, 1992); James Walvin, *Black Ivory: A History of British Slavery* (Malden, MA: Blackwell Publishers, 1992).

For colonial religion, in general, see Randall Balmer, *A Perfect Babel of Confusion: Dutch Religion and English Culture in the Middle Colonies* (New York: Oxford University Press, 1989); Patricia U. Bonomi, *Under the Cope of Heaven: Religion, Society, and Politics in Colonial America* (New York: Oxford University Press, 1986); Jon Butler, *Awash in a Sea of Faith: Christianizing the American People* (Cambridge, MA: Harvard University Press, 1990); Michael J. Crawford, *Seasons of Grace: Colonial New England's Revival Tradition in Its British Context* (New York: Oxford University Press, 1991); Harry S. Stout, *The New England Soul: Preaching and Religious Culture in Colonial New England* (New York: Oxford University Press, 1986).

For the Great Awakening, see Sylvia R. Frey and Betty Wood, *Come Shouting to Zion: African American Protestantism in the American South and British Caribbean to 1830* (Chapel Hill: University of North Carolina Press, 1998); Timothy D. Hall, *Contested Boundaries: Itinerancy and the Reshaping of the Colonial American Religious World* (Durham, NC: Duke University Press, 1994); Rhys Isaac, *The Transformation of Virginia, 1740–1790* (Chapel Hill: University of North Carolina Press, 1982); Susan Juster, *Disorderly Women: Sexual Politics and Evangelicalism in Revolutionary New England* (Ithaca, NY: Cornell University Press, 1994); Frank Lambert, *Inventing the "Great Awakening"* (Princeton, NJ: Princeton University Press, 1999); Lambert, *"Pedlar in Divinity": George Whitefield and the Transatlantic Revivals, 1737–1770* (Princeton, NJ: Princeton University Press, 1994).

Chapter 8: Empires

For the colonial wars, see Fred Anderson, *A People's Army: Massachusetts Soldiers and Society in the Seven Years War* (Chapel Hill: University of North Carolina Press, 1984); Anderson, *Crucible of War: The Seven Years' War and the Fate of Empire in British North America, 1754–1766* (New York: Alfred A. Knopf, 2000); Eric Hinderaker, *The Two Hendricks: Unraveling a Mohawk Mystery* (Cambridge, MA: Harvard University Press, 2010); John Robert McNeill, *Atlantic Empires of France and Spain: Louisbourg and Havana, 1700–1763* (Chapel Hill: University of North Carolina Press, 1985); Timothy J. Shannon, *Indians and Colonists at the Crossroads of Empire: The Albany Congress of 1754* (Ithaca, NY: Cornell University Press, 2000); Ian K. Steele, *Warpaths: Invasions of North America* (New York: Oxford University Press, 1994).

For the war in the interior and the Indian rebellions, see Gregory Evans Dowd, *A Spirited Resistance: The North American Indian Struggle for Unity, 1745–1815* (Baltimore: Johns Hopkins University Press, 1992); Eric Hinderaker, *Elusive Empires: Constructing Colonialism in the Ohio Valley, 1673–1800* (New York: Cambridge University Press, 1997); James H. Merrell, *Into the American Woods: Negotiators on the Pennsylvania Frontier* (New York: W. W. Norton, 1999); Jane T. Merritt, *At the Crossroads: Indians and Empires on a Mid-Atlantic Frontier, 1700–1763* (Chapel Hill: University of North Carolina Press, 2003); David L. Preston, *The Texture of Contact: European and Indian Settler Communities on the Frontiers of Iroquoia, 1667–1783* (Lincoln: University of Nebraska Press, 2009); Peter Silver,

Our Savage Neighbors: How Indian War Transformed Early America
(New York: W. W. Norton, 2008); Richard White, *The Middle Ground:
Indians, Empires, and Republics in the Great Lakes Region, 1650–1815*
(New York: Cambridge University Press, 1991).

For the new strains on the empire, see Bernard Bailyn, *Voyagers
to the West: A Passage in the Peopling of America on the Eve of the
Revolution* (New York: Alfred A. Knopf, 1986); Richard L. Bushman,
King and People in Provincial Massachusetts (Chapel Hill: University
of North Carolina Press, 1985); Woody Holton, *Forced Founders:
Indians, Debtors, Slaves, and the Making of the American Revolution
in Virginia* (Chapel Hill: University of North Carolina Press, 1999);
Michael A. McDonell, *The Politics of War: Race, Class, and Conflict
in Revolutionary Virginia* (Chapel Hill: University of North Carolina
Press, 2007); Gary B. Nash, *The Urban Crucible: Social Change,
Political Consciousness, and the Origins of the American Revolution*
(Cambridge, MA: Harvard University Press, 1979); Gordon S. Wood,
The Radicalism of the American Revolution (New York: Alfred A.
Knopf, 1992).

For Russian Alaska, see Barbara Sweetland Smith and Redmond
J. Barnett, eds., *Russian America: The Forgotten Frontier* (Tacoma:
Washington State Historical Society, 1990).

For Spanish California, see Ramon A. Gutierrez and Richard J.
Orsi, eds., *Contested Eden: California Before the Gold Rush* (Berkeley:
University of California Press, 1998); Lisbeth Haas, *Conquests and
Historical Identities in California, 1769–1936* (Berkeley: University of
California Press, 1995); Steven W. Hackel, ed., *Alta California: Peoples
in Motion, Identities in Formation, 1769–1850* (Berkeley: University
of California Press, 2010); Hackel, *Children of Coyote, Missionaries of
Saint Francis: Indian-Spanish Relations in Colonial California, 1769–
1850* (Chapel Hill: University of North Carolina Press, 2005); Albert L.
Hurtado, *Indian Survival on the California Frontier* (New Haven, CT:
Yale University Press, 1988).

For Pacific exploration, see Stephen Haycox, James K. Barnett, and
Caedmon A. Liburd, eds., *Enlightenment and Exploration in the North
Pacific, 1741–1805* (Seattle: University of Washington Press, 1997);
Derek Howse, ed., *Background to Discovery: Pacific Exploration
from Dampier to Cook* (Berkeley: University of California Press,
1990); Lynne Withey, *Voyages of Discovery: Captain Cook and the
Exploration of the Pacific* (New York: Morrow, 1987).

For the creation and expansion of the United States, see Patrick
Griffin, *American Leviathan: Empire, Nation, and Revolutionary*

Frontier (New York: Hill and Wang, 2007); Andres Resendez, *Changing National Identities at the Frontier: Texas and New Mexico, 1800–1850* (New York: Cambridge University Press, 2005); Nancy Shoemaker, *A Strange Likeness: Becoming Red and White in Eighteenth-Century North America* (New York: Oxford University Press, 2004); Alan Taylor, *The Divided Ground: Indians, Settlers, and the Northern Borderland of the American Revolution* (New York: Alfred A. Knopf, 2006).

Index